The Art of
HELPING
in the 21st Century

Robert R. Carkhuff

EIGHTH EDITION

Published by: Human Resource Development Press, Inc.
22 Amherst Road,
Amherst, Massachusetts 01002
800-822-2801 (U.S. and Canada)
413-253-3488
413-253-3490 (Fax)
http://www.hrdpress.com

Eighth Edition

International Standard Book No. 0-87425-530-9

Production services by Anctil Virtual Office
Cover design by Eileen Klockars
Editorial services by Robie Grant

TABLE OF CONTENTS

ABOUT THE AUTHOR

Dr. Robert R. Carkhuff believes that all human growth and development begins with relating.

Dr. Carkhuff considers himself fortunate to have begun his own career in helping and human relations. He was the first to define the interpersonal core of all helping and human relationships in operational, and therefore achievable, terms. The so-called Carkhuff model is specifically the source of all current systematic approaches to interpersonal relating and, indeed, is generally the source of human resource development approaches.

Indeed, it is precisely this theme of Human Development that defines Carkhuff's lifework. It begins with the most profound step: relating interpersonally. It culminates in a series of spiraling explosions: empowering people to actualize their own human potential. It is in the context of this ongoing work that this eighth edition of *The Art of Helping* is presented!

DEDICATION

Dedicated to Ralph Bierman, Ph.D., one of the early and continuing contributors to the new paradigm for helping human and community resource development.

PROLOGUE

To the Reader Upon Opening This Book:

This is the eighth edition of The Art of Helping. *Here is the data. More than 500,000 copies have been sold over three decades. Literally, millions of people have been trained in helping skills. Many millions more have been recipients of these skills. The effects upon hundreds of thousands of these recipients have been researched. We are very pleased with the results.*

Perhaps the most important thing that I can say is this: "We have been an important part of an interpersonal skills revolution." This revolution began less than one-half century ago with the work of neo-Freudians like Sullivan, Horney, and Fromm, was continued by the Client-Centered and Existential Schools, and finally was adopted by the Behaviorist and Trait-and-Factor Schools. In 1957, less than 50 years ago, Rogers formulated "the necessary and sufficient conditions of therapeutic personality change": empathy, regard, congruence. We were so privileged to have these giants as our intellectual ancestors.

It was left to us to operationalize these dimensions. It is, after all, the technological manifestations of our concepts that move humankind to change. We were successful in developing the first documented systematic interpersonal skills, or IPS, programs. Contrary to earlier theorists like Rogers, this meant that the skills were operationally defined and therefore learnable and achievable. They made a difference in the lives of the helpers as well as in the lives of the helpees.

In 1971, we published the first IPS model in The Art of Helping. *The impact of this work has been dramatic. Before 1971, there were few references in the literature to skills of any kind, let alone interpersonal and helping skills. Since then, the references have become voluminous. Indeed, the words interpersonal and skills are linked together in a growthful embrace. To be sure, all other IPS programs, however packaged, are derived from this original source. We are as proud today of* The Art of Helping *as we were then.*

More importantly, The Art of Helping *served to introduce the terms "responding" and "relating." Before 1971, people almost never interacted with others by using the pronoun you, let alone statements such as "You feel ____" or "You feel ____ because ____." Since then, most productive dialogue has been based upon making interchangeable "You feel" responses. In other words, for the first time in human history, people actually began to relate consciously and skillfully by entering the frames of reference of others. Imagine that! Humankind survived millions of prehistoric years to live ten thousand years as supposedly civilized people, yet its members never learned to relate to one another. Perhaps that is why most of human history is so pathic.*

And this is precisely the point that I would like to conclude with! With relating, humans may empathically enter the experience of any phenomena—not just human experiences. They may generate more useful information, growthful people, thinking organizations, expanding markets, productive communities, resourceful environments, generative sciences, and even new universes. Anything and everything is possible! Without relating, nothing is possible!

So learn your lessons well. This may be the first step in a very long human journey. It has been for me. The life you save may be your civilization's!

Good luck,

Robert R. Carkhuff

ACKNOWLEDGEMENTS

I owe a continuous and unpayable debt of gratitude to my colleague and friend, Dr. Bernard G. Berenson, of the Center for Human Resource Development, American International College, where we first developed the interpersonal skills or IPS programs. Our thirty-five years of interdependent processing have been the source of my greatest learning and personal development.

I am particularly indebted to Don Benoit for his contributions to this edition. I am also indebted to the staff of the HRD Center at AIC for their continuing support: Debbie Anderson, Cindy Littlefield, Sue Mackler, Richard Muise. In addition, I am appreciative of the administrative assistance of Bernice Carkhuff, Robert W. Carkhuff, and the staff at HRD Press for this eighth edition of *The Art of Helping*.

September, 1999   R.R.C.
McLean, Virginia

1 Introduction

We are born with the potential to grow—no more, no less! Those of us who learn to actualize this potential will know lives of untold fullness and excitement. We will develop growth responses that will enable us to go anywhere and do anything. Those of us who do not learn to actualize this potential will know lives of waste and tragedy. The choice is ours.

1.
THE EVOLUTION OF HELPING MODELS

The greatest impact upon the evolution of helping in the 20th century has been human resource development, or HRD, models. For the first time, the HRD models gave us an image of human functionality.

Insodoing, these models enabled us to view the practice of helping in perspective: in terms of the living, learning and working functions which people must perform; in terms of the physical, emotional and intellectual resources dedicated to these functions; in terms of the conditioning, learning and generating processes which enable the resources to discharge the functions.

These HRD models guide our helping models. They empower us to respond to human potential, to enhance it through personalizing, to file it or release it, to initiate, to discover its own changeable destiny. These are the gifts of HRD; they enable the process of helping.

THE IMPACT OF HRD UPON HELPING

Although helping relationships of an informal nature have taken place throughout the history of humankind, formal helping approaches originated in the Industrial Age. Along with psychology and the social sciences, the helping approaches were oriented toward dealing with the changing human experience.

For ten thousand years, people had passed on traditional agrarian roles from generation to generation. Then suddenly, with the advent of the Industrial Age, the human conditions changed; moreover, the conditioned roles and responses that had given stability to society and that, indeed, had enabled the advancement of civilization no longer worked.

The Changing Human Condition

Work roles evolved from farming and herding to mechanical operations where humans served as extensions of machines. With these changes, education—formal and informal—was transformed from an essentially spiritual indoctrination to a scientific and technological orientation; moreover, living conditions changed as people moved from the towns and villages of isolated farming communities to expanding networks of sprawling cities.

CHANGING CONDITIONS IN LIVING, LEARNING AND WORKING

The changes were incessant as new technologies emerged. Old workers were discarded from declining industries while new workers were demanded by emerging industries. Extended families, once the cornerstone of the old order, were torn apart by the mobility requirements of the new age. Schools were increasingly attuned to the changing requirements: people simply had to learn the basic skills involved in running, and being run by, machines. People needed to learn new responses to live, learn and work in the changing environment of the Industrial Age. As a result, the human condition was changed forever. Never again would it enjoy the stability of the traditional roles that had undergirded its security.

CHANGING RESPONSES TO CHANGING CONDITIONS

With advances in transportation and communications, the world has become "smaller." Now, in the Information Age, new roles and relationships are negotiated daily as people battle competitively for new opportunities and for the skills to take advantage of the opportunities. Some of the world's citizens are left behind in the wake of often crude social systems. Even the members of the middle class feel increasingly betrayed as contract after contract is broken: comfort is no longer assured; hard work does not yield security; career ladders no longer run up or even sideways. Stripped of their former roles, people, at some point in their lives, begin to search within themselves for the answer to the basic question of human experience: "Who am I?"

THE CHANGING HUMAN EXPERIENCE

Changing Approaches in Helping

As people began to examine their changing human experience, early helping approaches were created to facilitate this examination. Freud and the psychoanalysts viewed adult behavior in terms of early childhood experiences. Watson and the behaviorists viewed adult behavior in terms of early childhood conditioning. While these paradigms were similar, their treatment orientations differed greatly.

HELPING APPROACHES

The psychoanalytic, neo-analytic, client-centered, existential, and other treatment approaches that followed favored the *insight* approach. They believed that with insight, the helpees would function more effectively. In turn, the behavioristic, neo-behavioristic, trait-and-factor and other treatment approaches that followed favored action. They believed that with the conditioning of new and more effective responses, and/or the counter-conditioning of old and ineffective responses, helpees would function more effectively. To the proponents of these approaches, however, insight and action were unrelated or exclusive of each other.

INSIGHT/ACTION

INSIGHT OR ACTION

With the evolution of social learning theory, practitioners began to realize that the insight and action orientations were not as independently related as they had once assumed. Whether they began with human behavior or with insight, practitioners found that feedback from the practice of helping and research into the effectiveness of helping strategies moved them toward one another. They discovered that insights may be followed by programmatically developed actions in order for the helpee to function more effectively. Similarly, actions may be consolidated with insights. Indeed, personal growth and development in life may be seen in this paradigm: insight ⟶ action ⟶ insight ⟶ action (ad infinitum)

INSIGHT ⟷ ACTION

INSIGHT AND ACTION

With the introduction of human resource development models, we could view helping in perspective. The synergistic processing partners of insight and action were both dedicated to HRD: improving the performance of helpees on indices of physical, emotional and intellectual functioning. Indeed, at the highest levels, HRD defined health. And helping defined the insight–action approaches which empowered healthful functioning.

HRD
INSIGHT ⟷ ACTION

Human Resource Development

Human resource development, or HRD, is defined by its component resources: physical, emotional, intellectual. These resources are dedicated to functioning effectively to meet the requirements for the worlds in which we live, learn and work. These resources are enabled by the processes in which we engage: conditioned responding, discriminative learning, generative processing. Together, these functions, components and processes define HRD.

We may view the functions that we seek to discharge. First, we learn to live effectively in our worlds by relating to our environments and the people in them. Next, we learn to learn effectively by exploring, understanding and acting upon our worlds. Finally, we learn to work productively by performing or applying the skills, knowledge and attitudes that we have acquired.

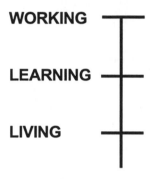

WORKING

LEARNING

LIVING

HRD FUNCTIONS

In turn, we may view the resource components that are dedicated to these living, learning and working functions. Physically, we must attain a level of fitness which supplies us with the energy to function effectively. Emotionally, we must be motivated and related to the functions. Intellectually, we must process in order to accomplish the functions. As may be seen, all resource components relate to all human functions in this 2D HRD matrix.

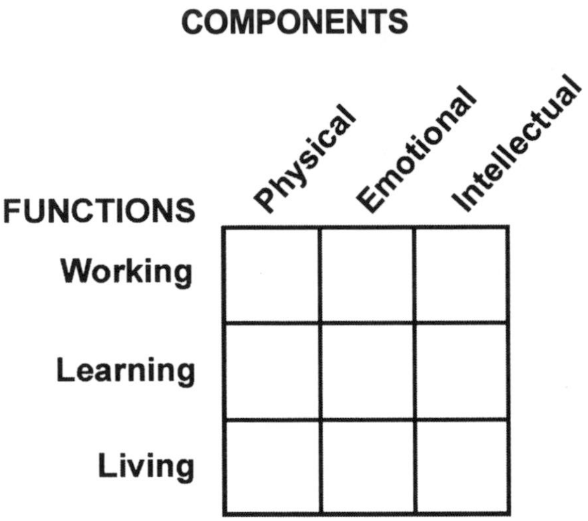

COMPONENTS

	Physical	Emotional	Intellectual
Working			
Learning			
Living			

FUNCTIONS

HRD COMPONENTS

Finally, we may view the human processes in which we must engage in order to enable the resource components to discharge the human functions. First, we have our basic S–R conditioned responding systems. Next, we have our S–O–R discriminative learning systems in which the S–R systems are "nested." Lastly, we have our S–P–R generative processing systems in which our S–O–R systems are "nested." As may be seen, all human processes relate to all resource components and all human functions in this 3D HRD model.

COMPONENTS

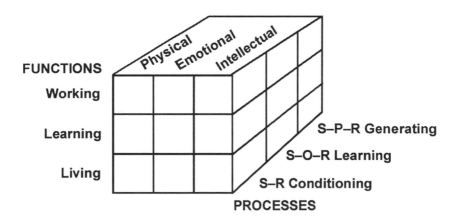

HRD PROCESSES

This, then, is the HRD model which will guide our helping efforts: living, learning and working functions discharged by physical, emotional and intellectual resource components enabled by conditioning, learning and generating processes. The HRD model is the key to personalizing problems and goals which is the focus of the helping process. The HRD model will empower us to diagnose current levels of functioning and set objectives for future levels of functioning in helping.

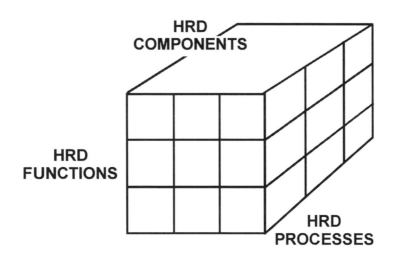

THE HRD MODEL

The Evolution of the Helping Model

Breakthroughs in helping came from research data on helping effectiveness. Basically, helping effectiveness could be accounted for by two factors: responding and initiating.

The responding factor involved the helper entering the helpee's frame of reference and accurately communicating an understanding of the helpee's experiences. The responding factor emphasized such dimensions as helper empathy or sensitivity, respect or warmth, and, sometimes, concreteness or specificity in focusing the helpee's experiences. If helpers could behave responsively, they could facilitate the helpees' exploration of their experiences and the development of insight.

HELPER: Responding

HELPEE: EXPLORING
(Insight)

HELPER RESPONDING ➜ HELPEE EXPLORING

In turn, the initiating factor involved developing a course of action to resolve the helpees' problems. The initiative factor emphasized action-oriented helper dimensions: genuineness or authenticity; self-disclosure or helper sharing of personal revelations; concreteness or specificity in problem solving and program development; and, under specifiable conditions, helper confrontations of discrepancies in helpee behaviors. If the helpers could behave initiatively, they could facilitate the helpees' acting on their problems and reaching their goals.

The responding and initiating dimensions worked together to facilitate the movement from insight to action in the helping process.

HELPER: Responding   Initiating

HELPEE: EXPLORING   ACTING
              (Insight)   (Action)

HELPER INITIATING ➞ HELPEE ACTING

Shaped by extensive research and demonstrations in living, learning and working contexts, the helping process was further refined. Personalizing skills involved filtering the helpee's experiences through the helper's experiences, and served (1) to facilitate helpee understanding and (2) to mediate between helper responding and initiating. These core helping skills facilitate the helpees' movement through the phases of *exploring* where they are in relation to their experience, *understanding* where they are in relation to where they want or need to be, and *acting* to get from where they are to where they want or need to be.

PHASES OF HELPING

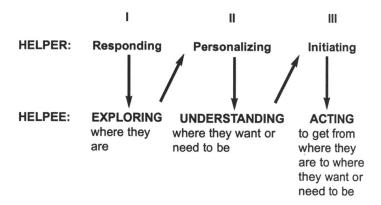

HELPER PERSONALIZING ➔
HELPEE UNDERSTANDING

The pre-helping attending skills completed the helping model. Attending to the helpees involved physical attending, observing and listening skills, and facilitated their involvement in the helping process. The helpers engage the helpees by giving them undivided attention. Helpee involvement triggers helper responding, thus facilitating exploring. In turn, helpee exploring enables helper personalizing of helpee understanding. Finally, helpee understanding activates helper initiating to facilitate helpee action.

PHASES OF HELPING

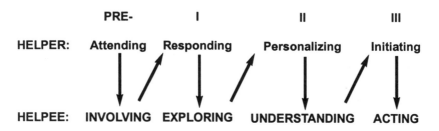

	PRE-	I	II	III
HELPER:	Attending	Responding	Personalizing	Initiating
HELPEE:	INVOLVING	EXPLORING	UNDERSTANDING	ACTING

HELPER ATTENDING → HELPEE INVOLVEMENT

Summary

With feedback, the phases of helping are recycled or revisited. The helpees receive feedback as a result of their acting. This feedback is recycled to stimulate more extensive exploring, more accurate understanding, and more productive acting. The purpose of helping is to engage the helpee in processes leading to human growth and development.

PHASES OF HELPING

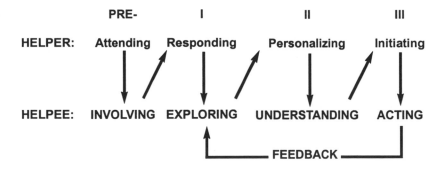

THE HELPING PROCESS

2

The Helping Process

The ingredients of a helping relationship are the skills and information the participants bring with them. The helpees bring with them their history of experience and their current abilities to "process"—both cognitively and affectively. The helpers bring to helping their own experiences and their "processing" skills—both cognitive and affective.

Together, helpers and helpees interact to facilitate their mutual "processing"—exploring, understanding, acting—of the helpees' problems and goals. This is the essence of helping.

2.
THE HELPEE'S CONTRIBUTION—
*INTRA*PERSONAL PROCESSING

The Age of Information brings with it extraordinary demands upon our abilities to "process" information. Not only are the information inputs of human experience constantly changing, they are also expanding exponentially. This means that many people become helpees because they are overwhelmed by the flood of information in their lives. For many, this feeling of being overwhelmed is the very reason that they seek help in the first place. Within helping, helpees "process" the information that they are unable to "process" outside of helping.

HELPEE PROCESSING

Helpee "processing" is a personal or *intra*personal process. The helpee relates to personally relevant experiences and transforms these human experiences into human actions for human purposes. *Intra*personal processing involves a basic set of skills: exploring human experience, understanding human goals, and acting upon programs to achieve the goals. Later on we may learn to teach the helpees systematic *intra*personal processing skills. For now, as helpers, we will learn interpersonal processing skills or helping skills to facilitate the helpees movement through these phases of *intra*personal processing—exploring, understanding and acting.

PHASES OF *INTRA*PERSONAL PROCESSING

	I	II	III
HELPEE:	EXPLORING ➤	UNDERSTANDING ➤	ACTING
	Human	Human	upon
	Experience	Goals	Programs

PHASES OF *INTRA*PERSONAL PROCESSING

Involvement in Processing

Before the helpees can process their experiences or explore, understand and act on them, they must be involved. Involvement means that they are prepared for processing by giving their undivided attention to personally relevant experiences. When helpees are prepared for processing with others, they are prepared to communicate their experiences.

The helpees prepare to involve themselves by focusing their attention upon their experiences. First, they bring into focus their values, or the meanings that they attach to things, by looking within themselves. They may begin by asking themselves about their reasons for seeking help. Their values may focus upon handling some difficult situation or opportunity. This becomes their goal in seeking help. The helpees begin involvement in processing by focusing upon some particular area of living, learning or working.

PHASES OF *INTRA*PERSONAL PROCESSING

PRE-HELPING

HELPEE: **INVOLVING**

HELPEE INVOLVEMENT IN PROCESSING

Exploring Human Experiences

Involvement leads to exploring human experience. Exploring means that the helpees are looking within themselves in order to determine where they are in relation to their experiences. They are focusing their thoughts and emotions upon those experiences that are relevant to their values and intentions. The helpees explore where they are so that they can understand where they want to be or need to be.

We observe the helpees exploring when they communicate personally relevant experiences. At high levels of exploring, the helpees share personally relevant experiences with emotional immediacy: they communicate what is important to them at that very moment. At high levels, the helpees also share their experiences with specificity: they detail the experiences they are expressing. At high levels of exploration, helpees explore themselves by experiencing themselves accurately. Exploration is, by definition, personally relevant, experienced with immediacy, and expressed with specificity.

PHASES OF *INTRA*PERSONAL PROCESSING

PRE- I

HELPEE: INVOLVING➤EXPLORING

HELPEE EXPLORING HUMAN EXPERIENCE

Understanding Human Goals

Exploring human experience leads to understanding human goals. Understanding means that the helpees are searching to see the implications of their experiences, identifying their problems, and defining their goals. Ultimately they are focusing their processing to generate remedies for their problems. The helpees attempt to understand where they want to be or need to be so that they can act to get there.

We observe helpees understanding when they describe the meaning of their experiences. Helpees show their level of understanding when they describe their problems and describe their role in their problems. At high levels of understanding, the helpees have clearly focused goals. This means that they have expanded alternative courses of action available to them before narrowing to preferred courses of action. They may expand courses by brainstorming or by systematically generating options. They may narrow courses by evaluating them in terms of their personal values and/or according to the requirements their environments impose upon them. At high levels of understanding, the helpees understand themselves with a high degree of accuracy.

√PHASES OF *INTRA*PERSONAL PROCESSING

	PRE-	I	II
HELPEE:	INVOLVING→	EXPLORING→	UNDERSTANDING

HELPEE UNDERSTANDING HUMAN GOALS

Acting upon Programs

In turn, understanding human goals leads to acting upon programs to achieve the goals. Acting means that the helpees are planning and implementing action steps. The helpees are focusing their actions upon living effectively in their real-life contexts. The helpees act to get from where they are to where they want or need to be.

We observe the helpees acting when they design plans and take action steps to achieve their goals. Acting involves defining specific performance objectives, developing detailed programs to achieve those objectives, and implementing the steps of the program. In this manner, the helpees act programmatically.

PHASES OF *INTRA*PERSONAL PROCESSING

	PRE-	I	II	III
HELPEE:	INVOLVING→	EXPLORING→	UNDERSTANDING→	ACTING

HELPEE ACTING UPON PROGRAMS

Feedbacking Information

*Intra*personal processing—exploring, understanding and acting—is incomplete until feedback from acting is recycled. Feedback information is received and reprocessed as new input to the *intra*personal processing system. It serves to generate more extensive exploring of human experience, more accurate understanding of human goals, and more productive acting upon human programs.

Feedback should be relevant to the helping goal. That is to say, the feedback provides information about their levels of performance. Feedback provides information relevant to the original helping goal.

PHASES OF *INTRA*PERSONAL PROCESSING

HELPEE FEEDBACKING OF INFORMATION

Summary

*Intra*personal processing—exploring, understanding and acting—describes the processes for all human growth and development. As helpers, our goal is to facilitate this process. Ultimately the goal of helping is to empower our helpees to explore, understand and act effectively without our help. All human growth and development involves a continual recycling of "processing—transforming human experience into human actions for human purposes—in an expanding spiral of human growth.

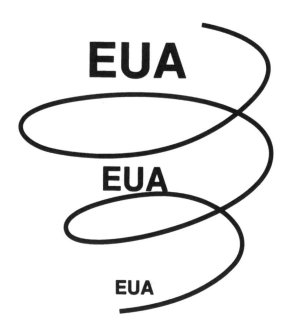

HELPEE *INTRAPERSONAL PROCESSING*—▶
HELPEE GROWTH

3.
THE HELPER'S CONTRIBUTION— INTERPERSONAL PROCESSING

The basic tenet of the Age of Information is inter-dependency. This means that we are each dependent upon the other. In this context, the basic helping skills in the Age of Information remain the interpersonal processing skills or helping skills. They enable a person to relate to the experiences of others. Helping skills or interpersonal processing skills facilitate the *intra*personal processing of others.

Interpersonal processing skills include attending skills to involve the helpees in the helping process. Responding skills facilitate exploring by the helpees. Personalizing skills facilitate understanding by the helpees. Initiating skills stimulate acting by the helpees. Feedback from the helpees' actions recycles the phases of *intra*personal and interpersonal processing.

PHASES OF INTERPERSONAL PROCESSING

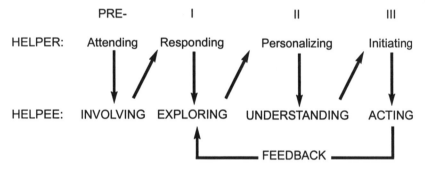

HELPER INTERPERSONAL PROCESSING SKILLS

Attending to Facilitate Involvement

During the pre-processing stage, the helpers attend or give attention to the helpees in order to involve them in the helping process. Attending involves communicating a hovering or undivided attentiveness to the helpees. Attending serves to focus the helpers' observing and listening skills upon the helpees' verbal and behavioral expressions of their experiences. These attending skills focus helping upon the helpees' experiences. Attending also serves to communicate an intense interest in the experiences of the helpees and so motivates them to become involved in the helping process.

PHASES OF INTERPERSONAL PROCESSING

PRE-HELPING

HELPER: **ATTENDING**

HELPEE: Involving

HELPER ATTENDING ⟶ HELPEE INVOLVEMENT

The basic attending skills are attending physically, observing and listening. Helpers attend physically so that they can observe. In turn, they observe so that they can listen. Attending physically emphasizes facing, squaring, leaning toward and making eye contact with the helpees. Observing emphasizes viewing the appearance and behavior of the helpees. Listening emphasizes "hearing" the content and the affect, or feelings, of the helpees' expressions of their experiences.

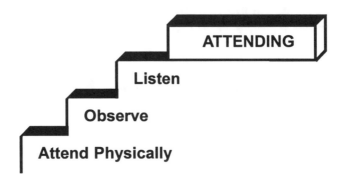

HELPER ATTENDING—ATTENDING PHYSICALLY, OBSERVING AND LISTENING

Responding to Facilitate Exploring

During the initial phase of the helping process, the helpers communicate statements that are "interchangeable" with the experiences of the helpee. Accurate responsiveness will serve to facilitate or stimulate the further exploration of the helpees' experiences.

PHASES OF INTERPERSONAL PROCESSING

I

HELPER: RESPONDING

↓

HELPEE: Exploring

HELPER RESPONDING ➝ HELPEE EXPLORING

The helpers "respond to the content" of the helpees' expressions by reflecting or communicating back to the helpees what they are saying or talking about. The helpers "respond to the affect" involved by reflecting how the helpees feel about what they are saying. Finally, the helpers may put the feeling and content together in a response that reflects the "meaning" of the experiences for the helpees. When accurate, these responses will facilitate further exploration of experiences by the helpees.

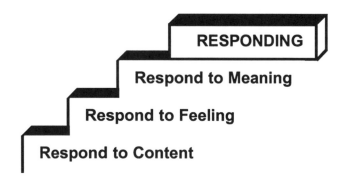

**HELPER RESPONDING—TO CONTENT,
FEELING AND MEANING**

Personalizing to Facilitate Understanding

During this transitional phase of the helping process, between responding and initiating, the helpers assist helpees in personalizing or internalizing their understanding of their experiences. The helpers go beyond communicating "inter-changeable" responses. The helpers draw from their own understanding to expand the helpees' understanding of the meaning of their experiences. The helpers facilitate the helpees in understanding and taking personal responsibility for their experiences. Personalizing also enables the helpees to define their problems and to transform their problems into goals.

PHASES OF INTERPERSONAL PROCESSING

II

HELPER: **PERSONALIZING**

HELPEE: **Understanding**

HELPER PERSONALIZING ➝
HELPEE UNDERSTANDING

The helpers assist the helpees in understanding the meaning of their experiences by communicating assumptions and implications in the form of "personalized meaning" responses. Helpers formulate and communicate a personalized description of the helpees' problems and assist the helpees in internalizing "responsibility for" or "ownership of" their problems. Helpers then formulate and communicate a personalized description of the helpees' goals and assist them in internalizing responsibility for achieving these goals. When accurate, these personalized responses will facilitate the helpees in accurately understanding, and taking responsibility for, their role in their problems and goals.

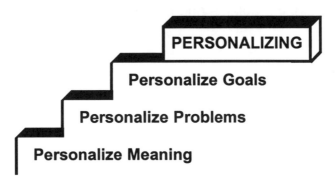

PERSONALIZING

Personalize Goals

Personalize Problems

Personalize Meaning

**HELPER PERSONALIZING—
MEANING, PROBLEMS AND GOALS**

Initiating to Facilitate Acting

During the culminating phase of the helping process, initiating, helpers assist the helpees to develop programs upon which the helpees can act. The helpers assist in further defining the personalized goals. They then assist in developing action programs to achieve these goals. Finally, the helpees implement these programs to resolve their problems and achieve their goals. Initiating by the helpers enables the helpees to culminate the helping process with action programs.

PHASES OF INTERPERSONAL PROCESSING

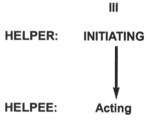

III

HELPER: INITIATING

HELPEE: Acting

HELPER INITIATING ➔ HELPEE ACTING

The helpers begin to initiate by defining specific goals with the helpees. The helpers continue to initiate in the development of action programs by defining the tasks and steps needed to achieve these goals. The next step in initiating is designing schedules or timetables and determining reinforcements. The helpers then prepare the helpees to implement their programs and plan check steps to provide feedback along the way. Initiating facilitates the helpees acting to achieve goals.

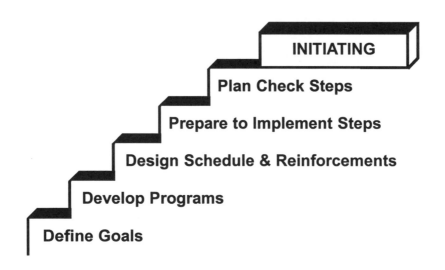

HELPER INITIATING—GOALS, PROGRAMS, SCHEDULES, REINFORCEMENTS, IMPLEMENTATION AND CHECK STEPS

Facilitating Feedback

Finally, the helpers will facilitate the feedbacking of information. The emphasis of feedback is upon the effectiveness of the helpees' action responses. If the helpees are satisfied with their action responses, then they may conclude this area of helping. If the helpees are not satisfied, then they may recycle their processing.

PHASES OF INTERPERSONAL PROCESSING

HELPER: FEEDBACKING

HELPEE: Recycling

HELPER FEEDBACKING ➝ HELPEE RECYCLING

The helpers gather performance information, then communicate this information to the helpees. The purpose of communicating this information is to tell the helpees how well they performed their responses. Information feedback serves as input to the helpees, assisting them in comparing their actual performance with their planned performance.

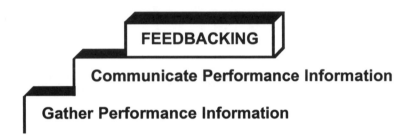

FEEDBACKING

Communicate Performance Information

Gather Performance Information

PROVIDING PERFORMANCE INFORMATION

Summary

As we enter this learning experience, remember that helping is a life-long journey. We help someone to grow and, in so doing, we grow ourselves. We empower helpees to become helpers and, in so doing, they grow themselves. In learning helping skills, emphasize becoming "one" with the helpees: do not let the skills get in the way of seeing the world through their experience. As much as anything else, helping is a change in our conditioned *"mindsets"*: from the terror of dependency (and the myth of independency) to the truth of interdependency; from victimization to actualization; from survival to growth; from helpee to helper. In the simple words of Dr. Berenson, *"Helping is the civilized thing to do."*

HELPER GROWTH ➞ HELPEE GROWTH

3

Helping Skills

The first year of human development serves as a prototype for all human learning. Initially, children explore and identify the nature of specific stimuli and responses. Later, children come to understand the interactive nature of stimuli and responses, anticipate the effect of one upon the other, and develop goals to achieve these effects. Finally, children act by drawing from their developing repertoire of responses to attempt to achieve their goals. Children's behavior is shaped by the feedback they achieve in their environments. This feedback recycles the stages or phases of learning as children explore more extensively, understand more accurately, and act more effectively. This ascending, enlarging spiral of exploring, understanding and acting is the source of every growing person's improving repertoire of responses.

4.
ATTENDING—INVOLVING THE HELPEE

"You can't get there from here." Behaviorally, the simplest step, attending, is also the step where most people fall down. Our entire cultural conditioning teaches us not to attend. That way we will not let our personal involvement get in the way of what we have to do to our *"competition."* By not attending, we communicate that others do not matter. We also fail to learn what it is they have to offer. Inevitably, non-attending is self-defeating. We are all losers!

NON-ATTENDING ➝ NON-ATTENTIVENESS

"You can't get there without it." The significance of attending is that we cannot help without it. In its broadest sense, it simply means *"paying attention."* By the principle of reciprocity, it means that people to whom we attend will, in return, attend to us. In other words, we communicate our interest in each other and the problem at hand. Now, attending has profound implications. My friend, Dr. Berenson, used to recommend that we assign counselor trainees an animal or a plant to keep alive for a year before working with humans. When we think about the requirements of animal and plant life, we begin to understand those of human life.

ATTENDING ⟶ PAYING ATTENTION

But the real function of paying attention is learning. We can learn most of what we need to know about any phenomena—human or otherwise—by using our senses as *"dedicated processors."* If you want to understand how one data element relates to another, then become one. If you need to understand an animal's frame of reference, then get on your hands and knees and view the world the way an animal does. If you want to understand human experience, then try becoming one—at least for a while! Assume the posture of the batter: *"Is the child trying to hit the ball or get out of its way?"* Observe the appearance of the learner: *"Is the student focused upon the learning material or upon disappearing into the woodwork?"* Listen to the grumblings of your peers: *"Are they talking about what they seem to be talking about or are they actually talking about themselves in relation to you?"*

PAYING ATTENTION ➔ HUMAN LEARNING

Now think about what you can learn from the appearance and behavior of your helpees. There are only three behavioral courses open to any person at any choice point in their lives: *flight, fight or relate:*

- *Flight* — Are they moving away from you?
- *Fight* — Are they moving against you?
- *Relate* — Are they moving toward you?

Are your helpees inclined to flight? Most are! Can you find the clues in their appearance and behavior? Are your helpees disposed to fight? Some are! What are the cues, or signals, of aggression? Are your helpees ready to relate? Few are! Their progress depends upon your skills.

HUMAN LEARNING ➞ HUMAN RELATING

Attending is the necessary precondition of helping. To experience its critical nature, turn away from others in your presence; then ask yourself, "Am I communicating interest in the others?" A more important question follows: "How do I learn about others or from others?" As you gradually turn back toward the others, you will learn about them. You will learn primarily by what you see and what you hear.

Attending skills posture the helper to see and hear the helpees. These skills involve preparing for attending, attending personally, observing and listening. Attending skills serve to involve the helpees in the helping process. When the helper is fully attentive, the helpees too may become fully attentive and engaged in the helping process.

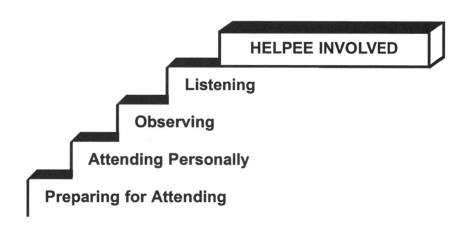

ATTENDING INVOLVES THE HELPEE

Preparing for Attending

The first task in attending is preparing for attending. Preparing for attending involves preparing the helpees, the context and the helpers. If the helpees are not prepared to make the contact, they will not appear. If the context is not prepared to receive the helpees, they will not return. If the helper is not prepared to attend to the helpees, they will not become involved in the helping process. Preparing for attending prepares us for attending personally to the helpees.

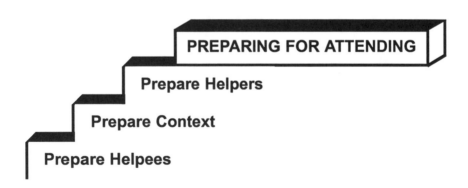

PREPARING FOR ATTENDING

Prepare Helpers

Prepare Context

Prepare Helpees

PREPARING FOR ATTENDING

The helpees' willingness to become involved will depend upon how well we prepare them for the helping interaction. Preparing the helpees involves *engaging* them, *informing* them of our availability, and *encouraging* them to use our help.

Engaging the helpees emphasizes greeting them formally and establishing a common frame of reference concerning the purpose of the contact.

Informing the helpees emphasizes communicating: **who** they will be seeing; **what** the general purpose of the contact will be; **when** and **where** the appointments will take place; and **how** to get there.

Encouraging the helpees emphasizes providing the helpees with the reasons for becoming involved by answering the following question: "Why do we want to get involved with each other?"

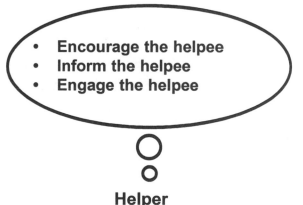

PREPARING THE HELPEE

Our ability to facilitate helpee involvement also depends in part upon preparing the context for the helpee. Preparing the context involves arranging furniture and decorations and organizing our offices or meeting rooms.

Arranging the furniture emphasizes facilitating open communication by positioning the chairs so that the helper and helpee face each other, with no desks, tables or other barriers between them. If there are several helpees, the chairs should be placed in a circle to facilitate the communication of interest and attentiveness to one another.

Arranging decorations emphasizes displaying decorations to which the helpees can relate—reflecting things that are familiar and comfortable to them.

Finally, the helping setting needs to be organized in a neat and orderly fashion. That way we communicate that we are on top of our own affairs and ready to focus upon the problems of the helpees.

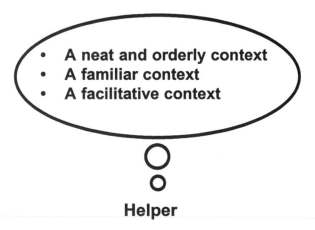

- **A neat and orderly context**
- **A familiar context**
- **A facilitative context**

Helper

PREPARING THE CONTEXT

It is as important to prepare ourselves for helping as it is to prepare our helpees and the context. We prepare ourselves by reviewing what we know about the helpees and the goal of helping as well as by relaxing ourselves.

Reviewing what we know about helping emphasizes reminding ourselves of what we know about the helpees from all previous interactions. This information may include formal notes, intake data and records, as well as informal impressions.

Reviewing the helping goals emphasizes the purpose of the contacts. For example, during the initial stages of helping, the goals will be to involve the helpees in exploring their experiences of their problems.

Relaxing ourselves emphasizes relaxing our minds and bodies prior to the actual helping interactions. Some helpers relax their minds by thinking of pleasant, soothing experiences. Others relax their bodies by physically relaxing one set of muscles after the other. We must experiment and find the method of relaxing that is most effective for us.

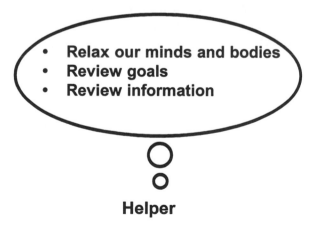

- **Relax our minds and bodies**
- **Review goals**
- **Review information**

Helper

PREPARING OURSELVES FOR HELPING

Attending Personally

By attending personally we bring our helpees into close proximity with us. In so doing, we communicate our interest in the helpees. Communicating an interest in the helpees tends to elicit a reciprocal response of interest from the helpees.

Attending personally involves posturing ourselves to give our full and undivided attention to the helpees. Attending personally emphasizes facing the helpees fully by squaring with them, leaning forward or toward them, and making eye contact with them. Attending personally to the helpees prepares us for observing them fully.

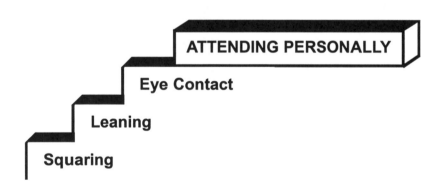

ATTENDING PERSONALLY

One way of posturing ourselves to attend to the helpees is to face them fully. Whether standing or sitting, we may attend to an individual helpee by facing him or her squarely— our left shoulder to the helpee's right shoulder and vice versa. When we are dealing with a couple or a small group of people, we should place ourselves at the point of a right angle drawn from the people to our extreme left and right. See how differently we feel about the helpees when we posture ourselves in this manner rather than posture ourselves primarily for purposes of our own comfort.

SQUARING

There are other ways of posturing ourselves to attend personally. The inclination of our bodies is another critical way. For example, when we are sitting we attend most fully when we incline our bodies forward or toward the helpees, to a point where we can rest our forearms on our thighs. When standing, we attend most fully when we close the physical distance by moving closer to the helpees. Putting one leg in front of the other will help us to lean slightly toward the helpees.

There are still other ways of attending to people in need of help.

LEANING

We must seek in every way possible to communicate our full and undivided attention. Perhaps the key way of attending personally involves how we use our senses, particularly our eyes. We communicate attentiveness when we maintain eye contact with the helpees. The helpees are aware of our efforts to make contact with them psychologically through our efforts to make contact with them visually.

MAKING EYE CONTACT

We may rate our level of "personal attending while sitting" by using the following scale.

High attending —Squared, eye contact, and leaning 20 degrees or more

Moderate attending —Squared, eye contact

Low attending —Not squared, slouching

LEVELS OF PERSONAL ATTENDING WHILE SITTING

Clearly, we do not always attend personally by sitting. Often we are attempting to help people while standing. We can use a similar scale to rate our demonstration of the skills while standing.

High attending —Squared, eye contact, and leaning 10 degrees

Moderate attending —Squared, eye contact

Low attending —Not squared

**LEVELS OF PERSONAL ATTENDING
WHILE STANDING**

We communicate personal attending by all of our mannerisms and expressions. When we are nervous and fidgety, we communicate a reluctance to be there. When we are intense but relaxed, we communicate attentiveness. When we are consistent in attentive behavior, we communicate interest. When we blush or turn pale, we communicate different levels of reaction to the helpees. It is important to have ourselves "together" in attending behavior.

We can practice our own attending posture, first in front of a mirror and then with people we see in everyday life, to whom we want to communicate interest and concern. We may feel awkward at first; after awhile, however, we should notice that we focus more upon the other person and that the other person is more attentive to us.

Perhaps the most important skill that personal attending prepares us for is observing.

**COMMUNICATING INTEREST—
CONSISTENT ATTENTIVE BEHAVIOR**

Observing

Observing skills are the most basic helping skills. They are a rich source of learning about the helpees. When all else fails, we emphasize observing our helpees. We learn much of what we need to know about people by observing them.

Observing skills involve the helper's ability to see and to understand the nonverbal behavior of the helpee. We must observe those aspects of the helpee's appearance and behavior which help us to infer the helpee's physical energy level, emotional feeling state and intellectual readiness for helping. These references are the bases for our initial understanding of where the helpee is coming from.

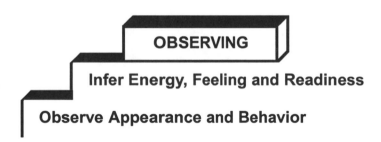

OBSERVING

When we observe we collect the nonverbal information that the helpees present to us. We learn about the helpees by noting their *appearance,* specifically their posture, body build and grooming. We can also collect information by observing their *behaviors,* specifically their facial expressions and body movements.

From their appearance and behaviors, we can make some inferences about their energy level, feeling state and readiness for helping.

- • **Observe body movements**
- • **Observe facial expressions**
- • **Observe grooming**
- • **Observe body build**
- • **Observe posture**

Helper

OBSERVING APPEARANCE AND BEHAVIOR

Energy level is the amount of physical effort put into purposeful tasks. Knowing how long people can sustain high levels of functioning is essential to knowing how people experience their lives. Only people with high energy levels can experience the fullness of life. Persons with low energy levels have great difficulty in meeting even the simplest demands of everyday life.

The richest source of information about energy level is communicated by the alertness of the helpee's posture. Specifically, the helper will look for the same cues in the helpee that were discussed earlier in helper attending: the extent to which the helpee stands and sits erect or leans forward with eyes focused on the helper. A helpee who sits slouched with shoulders drooped is taking a position that suggests low energy.

Energy level may also be expressed in body build. For example, helpees who are physically overweight or under-weight or have poor muscle tone will tend to have low levels of energy. Cues to the helpee's energy level can also be observed in grooming and nonverbal expressions. It takes a certain amount of energy to maintain a clean and neat appearance.

In addition to gathering information from appearance, helpee energy level can be inferred from helpee behavior. For example, slow helpee body movements may infer a low level of energy.

- **Observe grooming**
- **Observe body build**
- **Observe posture**

Helper
INFER PHYSICAL ENERGY

Facial expressions are the richest source of data concerning the helpee's feelings. Other areas, especially posture, also contribute to understanding the helpee's experience. Inferences can also be made based on body movements, with slow movements indicating "down" feelings and overly swift movements suggesting tension or anxiety. From this data we can infer the helpee's emotional feeling state. For example, a deep furrowed brow, a frown, a slouched posture, downcast eyes, poor grooming and slow body movements all communicate "down" feelings. A broad smile, raised eyebrows, an attending posture, eye contact, careful grooming and quick responsive body movements are associated with "up" feelings.

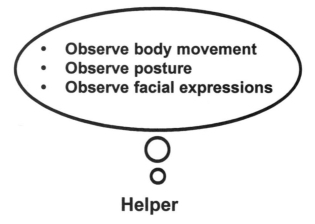

INFER EMOTIONAL FEELING STATE

From our observations of helpee appearance and behavior, we may infer their general intellectual readiness for helping. Again, helpee posture is the most powerful cue to readiness for involvement in helping. We can also learn about the helpee's readiness by observing body movements and facial expressions. A helpee who has a low energy level and "down" feelings will usually have a low readiness for helping, whereas a helpee with high energy and "up" feelings is usually ready for the helping process.

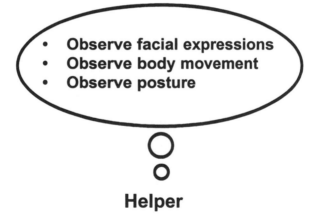

- **Observe facial expressions**
- **Observe body movement**
- **Observe posture**

Helper

INFER INTELLECTUAL READINESS FOR HELPING

By observing we can gain valuable information about the helpees' experiences. One way of structuring observing is to observe the helpees for precisely the same attending posture that we exhibit as helpers. Based upon our observations of appearance and behavior, we can make inferences about the helpees' functioning. We can infer a helpee's physical energy level, emotional feeling state and intellectual readiness for helping.

It is important to remember that observations must be considered hypotheses to be confirmed or denied over time by the helpees' behavioral and verbal expressions. Observations should not be taken as a valid basis for making snap judgments about a person.

INFERRING FROM OBSERVATIONS

Perhaps one of the most important aims of observation is identifying discrepancies or incongruencies in people's behavior or appearance. Being incongruent simply means that people are not consistent in their behavior or appearance. For example, people may be sitting slumped, looking at the floor and fidgeting, yet say they feel fine.

Being incongruent is itself a critical sign of people in trouble. Helpees invariably want to become more positively congruent. Perhaps the most important aspect of behavior to which you can respond initially is the helpees' desire to get themselves "together." More than anything else in the world, the helpees want to be able to function effectively without those glaring inconsistencies in their actions.

"I'm really feeling great!"

OBSERVING INCONGRUENCIES

We can observe ourselves in the same manner that we observe others. What does our appearance and behavior say about us? Do we project a high level of energy, feeling and readiness to help? Are we congruent in our behavior and our expressed desire to help?

We can also use our observations of ourselves and our helpees to involve the helpees. In helping, we should be focusing our entire beings upon the helpees and their expressions of their experiences. In this manner, we are communicating nonverbally that we are attending to them and that our interest is focused upon their experiences of themselves. In so doing, we increase the helpees' sense of comfort and security in helping.

OBSERVING OURSELVES

Listening

The sources of input that we most often rely on in helping are the verbal expressions of the helpees. What people say and how they say it tells us a lot about how they see themselves and the world around them. Ultimately, the helpees' verbal expressions are the richest source of empathic understanding for the helper.

When we give the helpees our full and undivided attention, we are prepared for listening to their verbal expressions. The more we attend to the external cues presented by the helpees, the more we can listen to the internal cues reflecting their inner experiences. There are many ways that we can develop our listening skills. These include having a reason for listening, suspending our judgment, focusing upon the helpee and the content, and recalling the helpees verbal and nonverbal expressions while listening for common themes. Listening prepares us for responding empathically to our helpees.

LISTENING

Recall Themes

Recall Expressions

Focus upon Helpee & Content

Suspend Judgement

Have a Reason for Listening

LISTENING

First, as listeners, we should know why we are listening. We should have a reason for listening. The goal of helping is the reason for listening—to gather information related to the problems or goals presented by the helpees.

As with observing, we should listen for cues that indicate the helpees' levels of physical, emotional and intellectual functioning. To do this, we must focus not only upon the words but also upon the tone of voice and the manner of presentation. The words will tell us the intellectual content of the helpees' experiences. The *tone of voice* will tell us about the helpees' attendant feelings. The *manner of presentation* will tell us about the helpees' energy levels. For example, content expressed in a dull tone of voice and in a listless manner suggests a depressed helpee with a low level of energy.

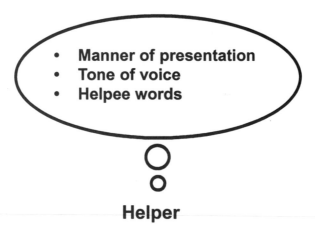

- **Manner of presentation**
- **Tone of voice**
- **Helpee words**

Helper

HAVING A REASON FOR LISTENING

Next, it is important to suspend our own personal judgments in listening, at least initially. If we are going to listen to what the helpees say, we must temporarily suspend the inner dialogue that we carry on with ourselves. We must let the helpees' messages sink in without trying to make decisions about them.

Suspending judgment means suspending our values and attitudes regarding the content of the helpees' expressions. For example, we may not approve of the helpees' behaviors or the ways they are living their lives. Our feelings, however, are not relevant to the helpees' experiences. Our purpose is to facilitate the helpees' growth and development. In addition, we must exercise caution in offering premature solutions, no matter how many times we think we have been over this ground with others. Each helpee has a unique experience, and it is our job to allow the uniqueness of that experience to emerge.

- **Suspend premature solutions**
- **Suspend personal attitudes**
- **Suspend personal values**

Helper

SUSPENDING PERSONAL JUDGMENT

Perhaps the most important thing in listening is to focus upon the helpees. We focus upon the helpees by resisting distractions. Just as we initially resist the judgmental voice within ourselves, so must we also resist outside distractions. There will always be a lot of other activities going on that will challenge our ability to listen.

We must place ourselves in quiet places so that we can focus upon the helpees' inner experiences. To the degree that we can, we must use a helping context that avoids noises, views and people—anything or anyone that will take our attention away from the helpees to whom we are listening. We must summon all of our energy, affect and intellect to focus upon the helpees' inner experiences and external behaviors so that we can respond accurately to those experiences and behaviors.

- **Focus on helpees' internal experiences**
- **Focus on helpees' external behaviors**
- **Resist distractions**

Helper

FOCUSING UPON THE HELPEES

In listening to the helpees, we focus initially upon the content. In focusing upon the content, we want to be sure that we have all of the details of the helpees' experiences; otherwise, we will not be able to help them to understand their experiences. We focus upon content by asking ourselves the 5WH basic interrogatives:

Who?
What?
Why?
When?
Where?
How?

If we can answer these questions, we can be sure that we have the basic ingredients of the content of the helpees' experiences. If we cannot answer these questions, we should continue to listen. As the helpees share their experiences, they will fill in the missing information for us.

FOCUSING UPON THE CONTENT

We should concentrate intensely enough upon the helpees' expressions to be able to recall both the content and the attendant affect of the helpees. In addition we also want to recall any gaps—missing information.

To practice your listening skills in recalling brief expressions, try to recall the entire expression verbatim. With lengthy expressions, try to recall the gist of it. After you read the following expression of a young man in trouble, try to recall the content, affect and any "gaps" in information.

> "Things are not going so good for me. Not in school. Not with my girl. I just seem to be floundering. I fake it every day, but inside I'm really down because I'm not sure of what I want to do or where I want to go."

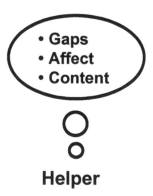

RECALLING THE EXPRESSION

We must also learn to recall the helpees' expressions over a period of time. In so doing, we are looking for the common themes in the helpees' experiences. The helpees' important themes will be repeated over and over. Usually, the helpees will invest the most intensity in these themes because they are trying to communicate them to us.

These themes will tell us what the helpees are really trying to say about themselves and their worlds. They will tell us where they are "coming from" if we just provide them the opportunity. We need only receive the messages they are sending and process them for their common themes. This will prepare us to respond accurately to the helpees.

We should practice listening for themes in our daily conversations. For now, we can use the case studies at the end of each chapter. See how well we do when compared to the helpers involved.

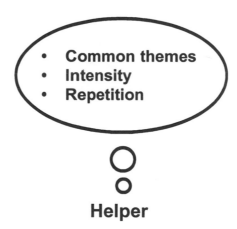

LISTENING FOR THEMES

There is no question that listening is hard work. It requires intense concentration. However, just as there are different rates for reading, there are different rates for listening. Most people talk at the rate of 100 to 150 words a minute, yet we can easily listen at a rate of two or three times that amount. We can put this extra time to use by reflecting upon or thinking about what the helpees have said.

Most of us have been taught not to listen or to hear. Years of conditioning have gone into this. We are distracted because we do not want to hear. We distort the expressions because of the implications of understanding. Most of all, there are the implications for intimacy that make people fearful. Just as we have been conditioned not to listen and not to hear, now we must train ourselves to listen actively and to hear the expressions of the helpees.

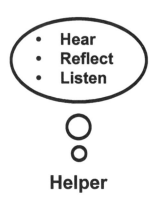

HEARING

Summary

One of the ways to measure our listening skills is to test our verbatim recall of the helpees' expressions. Simply listen to these expressions and try to repeat verbatim what you heard. We may practice in live interactions or with written or taped expressions. We may rate the accuracy of our recall as follows:

High accuracy —Verbatim recall of expression

Moderate accuracy —Recall of gist of expression

Low accuracy —Little or no recall of expression

In the end, the entire verbal helping process hangs on our ability to listen and to process the content and affect of the helpees' expressions.

LEVELS OF LISTENING

Now we can begin to build our own cumulative rating scale for helping. If the helper is attending personally, observing and listening to the helpees, we may rate the helper as fully attentive (level 2.0). If the helper is only attending personally (squaring, leaning, eye contact), then the helper is rated at a less than fully attentive level (level 1.5). If the helper is not attending personally, then the helper cannot be rated in relation to the helpee (level 1.0).

LEVELS OF HELPING

5.0
4.5
4.0
3.5
3.0
2.5
2.0   Observing and listening
1.5   Attending personally
1.0   Nonattending

LEVELS OF HELPING—ATTENDING

If we have attended to the helpees effectively, then we will have involved them in helping. The helpees will experience comfort in the preparations we made for them. They will experience security in our attentiveness. They will begin to share their experiences, and we will have the opportunity to listen and hear their expressions.

Above all else, the helpees will begin to reciprocate by involving themselves in the helping process. They will prepare for their sessions. They will become attentive and observant of themselves and others. They will begin to share their experiences and listen in turn to the expressions of others. In so doing, the helpees signal their readiness to enter the exploratory phase of helping.

PHASES OF HELPING

PRE-

HELPER: Attending

HELPEE: INVOLVING

FACILITATING INVOLVING

Like any other set of skills, you will want to practice the attending skills until you have integrated them into your helping personality as the helper in the following case study has done.

Case Study #1—Skilled Attending

Terry is a twenty-three-year-old male who is tall, broad-shouldered and muscular. Paula, a therapist, first met Terry in the waiting room outside her office. Her only preparation was a phone call, received from a company where she had a contract to provide employee assistance counseling, asking her for an emergency appointment for Terry that afternoon.

When Paula walked into the waiting room, she was surprised. Terry did not look like her typical client. He wore work clothes, clean but obviously used for their purpose. Moreover, he was agitated and angry, pacing back and forth, his face contorted with the effort of controlling his rage. After hesitating a fraction of a second, she approached him.

Paula: (reminding herself to stay relaxed)
"Good morning. You must be Mr. Mason."

Terry: "Yeah."

Paula: (extending her hand) "My name is Paula Rantoul." (Terry takes her hand with a grasp that threatens to smash her fingers but turns out to be just a firm handshake.) "Please come into my office. Take the chair by the window; it's the most comfortable." (As Terry sits down Paula offers a cup of coffee, which he refuses. Paula sits in a chair opposite Terry, leaning forward.) "Now, I understand you want to see me about some things that are troubling you."

Terry: "—damn right! I just lost by job because I hit my foreman! If I don't learn how to control my temper my whole life will turn to shit!" (Paula leans forward a little more and looks at Terry frankly.) "I don't know what a little girl like you can do to help me, but I'm ready to give anything a try!"

On he talked for another fifteen minutes, nonstop. Once he jumped up and started pacing, slamming his fist into his hand again and again as he talked. Paula stayed in her chair, turning to face him as he walked back and forth. When he realized what he was doing, he smiled sheepishly and sat back down. Finally he stopped his tirade and, sitting back in the chair, looked at Paula sitting across from him.

Terry: "You know, you got real guts. Most women would have hightailed it out of here or tried to get me to sit still. Why not you?"

Paula: (quietly, looking at Terry) "You don't need another person to be afraid of you, nor do you need a mother to criticize you right now. You said you want someone to help you. I've got to find out who you are first if I'm going to be that person. I can't do that if I'm running from you or trying to get you to do what I want."

Terry: (looking baffled for a minute, then smiling) "You really know what you're doing. You'll do."

Paula: (smiling back) "You're too strong to allow me to treat you like a child. You're too strong to allow yourself to act like a child."

Terry: "You know you're right. I don't want to be out of control. All it does is get me into trouble."

It took every one of Paula's attending skills to maintain contact with Terry. She had to attend contextually by preparing herself, the environment and Terry for the interaction. She did that by keeping her tension in control, putting Terry at ease, and by making her office as comfortable and yet as constructive as she could for her interaction with Terry. She made sure she kept good eye contact. She leaned forward and kept herself squared to Terry, even when he was pacing back and forth. She made observations that helped her to recognize that Terry was in control of his anger, but only barely. And she listened to what he was saying, trying to get information for future use.

Her efforts paid off. Her consistent use of attending skills resulted in having Terry commit himself to working with her, recognizing that she could help him grow.

Attending is a necessary but not sufficient condition of helping. It prepares us to relate to others. Indeed, by the principle of reciprocal affect, it initiates the relating process. The people we are working with will tend to relate to us the way we relate to them. If they do not, we will explore why!

ATTENDING ⟶ PREPARING FOR RELATING

5.
RESPONDING—FACILITATING EXPLORING

Yes, our cultural conditioning trained us to avoid relating. And it was wrong! Wrong because the so-called *"competitive ethic"* no longer works—and never was an ethic! Wrong because there is no such a thing as independence—never was, as any recently laid-off workers will testify! Wrong because things change! We were sold a lie in the 20th century. It said, *"Be independent and competitive people and the system will reward you."* We have found out otherwise. By not relating, we have not been related to. The system has rewarded us in kind by not relating to us.

NON-RELATING ➞ NON-RELATIONAL

In fact, the course of civilization lies straight ahead of us. We are preparing for a very complex world, a world of spiraling changes. This brave, new world brings with it a whole new set of requirements. Primary among these requirements is the ethic of interdependency. We will either live together or fall apart. We can only live together by relating, by cooperating and collaborating, by integrating. The theme of the 20th century was *"Compete or die!"* The theme of the 21st century is *"Relate or die!"*

RELATING ⟶ RELATIONAL

The function of relating is interdependence. Humans were always interdependently related to each other and their worlds. It was only *"humankind"*—a kind of human—that conceived of itself in independent terms. Interdependence means that we are each dependent upon the other, and all dependent upon this *"fragile spacecraft"* that we call Earth. It means relating—to merge with one another and the phenomena we are studying. It means becoming one with that phenomena and helping it to actualize its growth potential. And, in so doing, to actualize ours!

RELATING ➞ INTERDEPENDENCE

What interdependence does not mean is consensus-building or response sharing. Interdependence means becoming part of our worlds—our part, to be sure, but nevertheless part of something larger than ourselves. In the world of interdependence, everything matters. Everything that any one element does potentially relates to everything else in the world. Everything! It may be people. It may be data. It may be things. All of these relate within themselves as well as between and among themselves. That is how we integrate ourselves and our worlds. But we do so only if these things matter to us. Only if we want to help! Only if we have the skills to relate!

INTERDEPENDENCE → INTEGRATING

Responsive communication, or responding, facilitates the helpees' exploration of where they are in relation to their worlds. We attend, observe and listen to the helpees so that we can respond to them. Responding emphasizes entering the helpees' frames of reference and communicating to them what we hear and see. In other words, there are two separate sets of skills involved: *discriminating accurately* the dimensions of the helpees' experiences and *communicating accurately* to the helpees the dimensions we have perceived.

Responding involves responding to content, feeling and meaning. We *respond to content* in order to clarify the ingredients of the helpees' experiences. We *respond to feeling* in order to clarify the affect attached to the experience. We *respond to meaning* in order to clarify the reason for the feeling.

Responding facilitates helpee exploring. When the helper responds accurately to the helpees, then the helpees explore where they are in relation to their worlds. Responding both stimulates and reinforces helpee exploring. It lays the base for personalizing to facilitate helpee understanding.

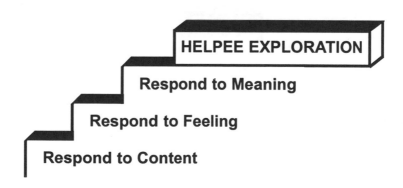

RESPONDING FACILITATES HELPEE EXPLORING

Responding to Content

We respond first to the most obvious part of the helpees' expressions—the content. We respond to content in order to clarify the critical ingredients of the helpees' experiences. Having an accurate content data base enables us to establish our responsive base in helping: responding to feeling and meaning. In turn, this responsive base will enable us to personalize understanding and initiate acting.

The ingredients of content emphasize the basic interrogatives, which may be summarized as 5WH: who, what, why, when, where, and how.

A good response rephrases the helpees' expressions in a fresh way. It does not simply "parrot" back the helpees' own words. A good format for responding to content is

"You're saying _____."

    or

"In other words, _____."

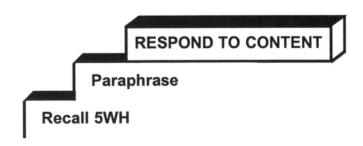

RESPOND TO CONTENT

Paraphrase

Recall 5WH

The basic interrogatives provide us with a format for testing the completeness of the helpees' expressions of their experiences. In other words, they enable us to determine whether the helpees have included everything we need to know. The interrogatives may be formulated as follows:

Who and **what** was involved?
What did they do?
Why and **how** did they do it?
When and **where** did they do it?

For example, we may examine the following expression for the interrogatives:

"I thought I had things together with my teacher."
(WHO)

"But now I flunked the exam." (WHAT)

*"I guess we were on different wavelengths.
I sure didn't expect questions that hard."* (WHY)

"I guess I didn't study enough (HOW)
at home before the test." (WHEN and WHERE)

RECALL 5WH

The 5WH helps us to organize details and know if the helpee is leaving out information. The response formulated by the helper, however, need not repeat the details. Rather, the helper, using his or her own words, will *paraphrase* the helpee's content by summarizing. A paraphrased response to content, in the form of a brief statement, will capture the main points communicated by the helpee.

"In other words, you overestimated where you were with the teacher and with your subjects."

Helper

PARAPHRASE CONTENT

Responding to the content facilitates the process by which the helpees continue exploration and provide missing information. If any of the 5WH interrogative information is not explored by the helpee, we will naturally want to probe the helpees to get a more complete picture of their experiences. To encourage helpee exploration, however, we must continue to respond and refrain from our initial reflex to ask a series of questions. For now, our focus is upon responding to what the helpees are saying, not what we want them to talk about. Later, we may find it expedient to ask some questions to fill certain gaps in our understanding. When we ask a question, it is best to follow it with a response. Indeed, the skilled helper will sandwich questions between two responses.

To respond to content, listen for the 5WH. These essential ingredients will enable us to later diagnose the helpees' deficits. We respond to content by organizing it and then communicating our understanding of it to the helpees.

We may wish to practice responding to content by doing so in real-life situations or through the use of recorded expressions. The case studies in this book may be helpful material for practicing formulating content responses.

FACILITATING EXPLORING OF CONTENT

Responding to Feeling

Just as we showed our empathy for the helpees by responding to the content of their expressions, we may show our understanding of their experiences by responding to the feelings that they express. Indeed, responding to content prepares us to respond to the feelings of the helpees' expressions. Responding to feelings is the most critical single skill in helping because it reflects the helpees' affective experience of themselves in relation to their worlds.

Helpees may express verbally and directly those feelings that dominate them, or the helpees may express their feelings indirectly, through their tone of voice or by describing the situation in which they find themselves.

Whether the helpees' expressions are direct or indirect, our goal, as helpers, will be to explicitly show the helpees our level of understanding of their feelings by formulating a response to their feelings. This will give the helpees a chance to check out our effectiveness as helpers. It will also give us a chance to check our own level of accuracy.

Responding to feelings involves asking and answering the empathy question and developing interchangeable responses to feelings.

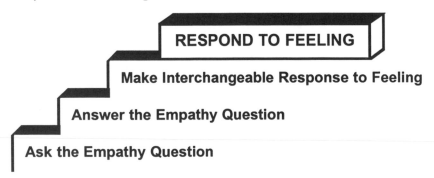

RESPOND TO FEELING

Make Interchangeable Response to Feeling

Answer the Empathy Question

Ask the Empathy Question

RESPONDING TO FEELING

To respond to the helpee's feelings, we must first observe personal behaviors. In particular, we must pay attention to tone of voice and postural and facial expressions. These self-expressions will tell us a great deal about how helpees experience themselves and will be valuable clues to their inner feelings.

Next we must listen carefully to the helpee's words. Now that we have observed and listened, we must summarize what we have seen and heard with a response that indicates the helpee's feelings. We do this by asking ourselves the question, "If I were the helpee and I were doing and saying these things, how would I feel?" In answering this question, we first identify the general feeling category (happy, angry, sad, confused, scared, strong or weak) and the intensity of the feeling (high, medium or low). Then we select a feeling word or phrase that fits the feeling category and level of intensity. Finally, we check the feeling expression with our observations to determine if it is appropriate for the helpee involved.

ASKING THE EMPATHY QUESTION

By answering the empathy question we try to understand the feelings expressed by our helpee. We summarize the cues to the helpee's feelings and then answer the empathy question "How would I feel if I were the helpee?" Let's ask and answer the empathy question about Tom.

> **Tom:** "Things are not going so good for me. Not in school. Not with my girl. I just seem to be floundering. I fake it every day, but inside I'm really down because I'm not sure of what I want to do or where I want to go."

The main cue to Tom's feelings is that he says he feels down. He's down about school and down about his relationship with his girl. He's also floundering. If we were in his position, we might very well feel sad.

To everyday life expressions, practice asking and answering the "How would I feel if I were the helpee?" question.

Helper

ANSWERING THE EMPATHY QUESTION

We can ensure that we respond to the helpee's feelings when we make a response that is interchangeable with the feelings expressed. It certainly is not too much to expect that we be able to communicate to the helpee what the helpee has communicated to us. Understanding what the helpee has expressed—at the level it was expressed to us—constitutes the basis of communication and makes helping possible.

A response is interchangeable with feelings if both the helper and the helpee express the same feeling.

The first response to feeling that we formulate should involve very simple feeling words to reflect the feelings expressed by the helpee. We may do this by using a simple "You feel _____" formulation. Before we move to more complex communication, we must learn to formulate simple responses.

We may say that we respond to the helpee's feelings when we capture and communicate the essence of the helpee's feelings in one or more feeling words.

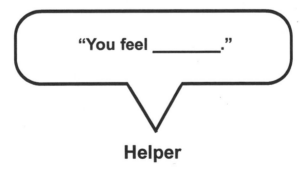

"You feel _____."

Helper

**DEVELOPING INTERCHANGEABLE
RESPONSES TO FEELINGS**

Now let's try to formulate a feeling response to a helpee's expression. Let's repeat Tom's expression again:

> "Things are not going so good for me. Not in school. Not with my girl. I just seem to be floundering. I fake it every day, but inside I'm really down because I'm not sure of what to do or where I want to go."

We ask ourselves, "How would I feel if I were Tom?" We answer, "Sad—I would feel sad." Now we formulate the response in a way that communicates directly how he feels: "You feel sad."

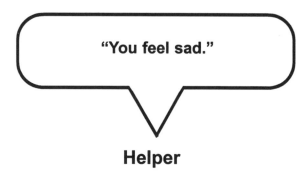

"You feel sad."

Helper

RESPONDING TO SAD FEELINGS

Helpees exhibit many different moods—many different feeling states. Sometimes they seem very sad. Sometimes they seem very happy. Sometimes they seem very angry. Most times they are somewhere in between these extremes.

We must have responses that communicate to them our understanding in each of these moments. We must be able to formulate simple and accurate responses to their feeling states.

For example, Tom is kind of sad or "down." His energy level appears low. Things seem pretty hopeless. He feels helpless in the face of everything. He just does not know where he is going. Tom verbalizes this feeling when he says, "Sometimes I just think that I'm not going to make it."

Using an appropriate feeling word for this kind of sadness, we might formulate a simple response.

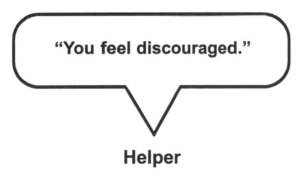

"You feel discouraged."

Helper

RESPONDING ACCURATELY TO SAD FEELINGS

In rare moments, our helpees might be "up," particularly when they have found some direction, however tentative. Their whole demeanor changes. Their attitude toward life opens up. Their behavior is intense and brisk.

It is just as important to be able to respond to the helpees in these "up" moments as it is to respond to them in their depressed moments. Indeed, it is ultimately more important to celebrate and reinforce joyful, positive experiences.

While it is critical to "meet" our helpees at the level that they are expressing themselves, we must ultimately help them to move to new and more rewarding behavior. We cannot help them to move if we cannot also respond to those rare moments of joy.

For many of us, these are the most difficult experiences to respond to. Sharing another's joy is difficult indeed for those of us whose own moments of joy are few and far between.

For example, sometimes Tom's feelings are so intense that he blurts them out: "I can't wait to get started!" We might formulate a simple response to his feeling state.

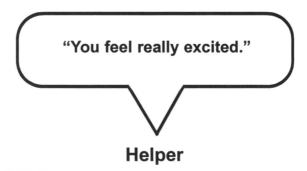

"You feel really excited."

Helper

RESPONDING ACCURATELY TO HAPPY FEELINGS

At times, the helpees might express other kinds of feelings, ones that might be difficult to respond to. Sometimes they are just mad at the world, angry with its injustice and motivated to retaliate. Their bodies are tense, their eyes tearing and their expressions choked. Often we are afraid to open up such feelings. We are afraid of how far these feelings may carry them. Will they act upon them? Will they act them out? These are the questions that characterize our concern.

Nevertheless, we cannot help if we cannot deal with all of a person's feelings. Suppose Tom, our helpee, has been treated unfairly by someone and is very upset. Our helpee must get these feelings out in the open if he is going to learn to deal with them. Indeed, the probability of his acting upon angry feelings is inversely related to his ability to explore them. The more he explores them, the less likely he is to act destructively. Put another way, the more he explores them, the more likely he is to channel them constructively. Sometimes he expresses his feelings in violent terms: "I know damn well I'm gonna get back at him any way I can!" We may formulate a simple response to him.

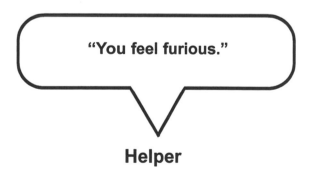

"You feel furious."

Helper

RESPONDING ACCURATELY TO ANGRY FEELINGS

We must respond to our helpees in all their fullness—in their moments of sadness, happiness and anger. They are how they feel. If we do not respond to our helpees in their fullness, the implications are clear: if we cannot find them, we lose them; if we lose them, they cannot find themselves.

There are many variations of feeling themes. Some major themes are surprise, fright, relief, distress, affection, disgust, interest and shame. There is a wide range of more specific feeling states to which we can respond. We must learn to respond to these unique feelings.

It is beneficial for both the helper and the helpee to struggle to capture in words the uniqueness of the helpee's experiences. Finding the most accurate feeling words may not be easy at first. You may say to yourself, "I just don't ordinarily use that many feeling words. I don't know if I can respond accurately." You will need to expand your feeling-word vocabulary.

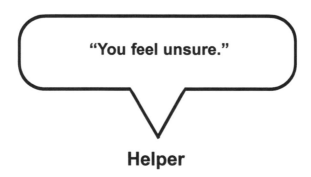

"You feel unsure."

Helper

RESPONDING TO UNIQUE FEELINGS

The more feeling words we have available to us, the better our chances of accurately communicating our understanding of the helpees and their unique experiences.

One effective way of organizing feeling words is to categorize them according to whether they are of high, medium, or low intensity. Since the intensity of any word depends upon the person with whom it is used, we will need to visualize the typical helpees we work with. Then we can determine both the feeling category and the level of intensity that we wish to employ. We may develop our own word list by filling in page 115. Appendix A contains an alphabetical listing of feeling words from which to draw. We may carry a list around with us and add to it. It will help us to learn to respond accurately.

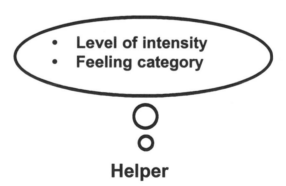

EXPANDING RESPONSES TO FEELING

Based upon the cues we receive from our observations and from the helpee's initial statements, we attempt to determine the "general feeling category" of the helpee's feelings. Our next task is to fine-tune our understanding of the helpee's feelings. We want to find feeling words that are interchangeable with our helpee's experience. If we are having difficulty finding the "right words" but know we are in the "ballpark," we can try the following technique.

We begin by simply completing this statement: "When I feel _____ (general feeling), I feel _____ (specific feeling)." This will help us to find a more accurate interchangeable response to feeling.

For example, if the helpee says, "I feel depressed," and we find ourselves at a loss for a new, more accurate word with which to respond, we might say to ourselves, "When I feel depressed, I feel _____." We might complete this statement with "lost." "When I feel depressed, I feel lost." Look at and listen to the helpee. Does the helpee look and sound "lost"?

We continue to recycle this process and check out new feeling words until we have found an interchangeable feeling word.

Helper

FINDING AN APPROPRIATE FEELING WORD

Categories of feelings

Levels of Intensity	Happy	Sad	Angry	Scared	Confused	Strong	Weak
High	Excited	Hopeless	Furious	Fearful	Bewildered	Potent	Overwhelmed
	Elated	Depressed	Seething	Afraid	Trapped	Super	Impotent
	Overjoyed	Devastated	Enraged	Threatened	Troubled	Powerful	Vulnerable
Medium	Cheerful	Upset	Agitated	Edgy	Disorganized	Energetic	Incapable
	Up	Distressed	Frustrated	Insecure	Mixed-up	Confident	Helpless
	Good	Sorry	Irritated	Uneasy	Awkward	Capable	Insecure
Low	Glad	Down	Uptight	Timid	Bothered	Sure	Shaky
	Content	Low	Dismayed	Unsure	Uncomfortable	Secure	Unsure
	Satisfied	Bad	Annoyed	Nervous	Undecided	Solid	Bored

*Since the intensity of any feeling word depends upon the person with whom it is used, you will need to visualize the typical helpee you work with to categorize these words by intensity level. (An Expanded Feeling Word List is found in Appendix A.)

The helpees' feelings are at the heart of their experience of the world. For better or worse, human feelings are perhaps the most fundamental characteristics of human experience. They are aroused by what we do and what is done to us; they are reflected in what we subsequently do and think; they condition how we act toward others and how we treat ourselves.

Our feelings and the feelings of our helpees are real—for better or worse. And it is with the helpees' feelings that the helper must relate.

We may wish to practice responding to feelings. We can respond to real-life situations or recordings. The case studies in this text and the exercises in the student workbook may provide helpful stimulus materials for practice in formulating feeling responses.

FACILITATING EXPLORING OF FEELING

Responding to Meaning

Responding to the feeling or the content of the helpees' expressions is not enough. Our response must be enriched by combining the feeling together with the content for the helpees.

Content is used to make the feeling meaningful. The content gives intellectual meaning to the helpees' expressions of their experiences. The feeling gives emotional meaning to the helpees' expressions of their experiences. Responding to meaning emphasizes making interchangeable responses that capture both the feeling and content of the expressions.

RESPONDING TO MEANING

Respond Interchangeably

Capture Content and Feeling

RESPONDING TO MEANING

Perhaps no other single construct is as fundamental to our understanding of daily life as the principle of cause and effect. Nothing occurs in a vacuum. There is a reason for every event that takes place. And every feeling, however elusive and insubstantial it may seem, is prompted by some specific cause or causes.

Many of our feelings seem quite rational in the sense that most other people would feel the same way if the same things happened to them. But we also have feelings that seem to make little or no sense to others. Whatever we see as the cause of our feelings may not appear sufficient when viewed by other people. In still other cases, we may not realize the cause for our feelings.

Helpers must remember this: *Regardless of the apparent nature of the cause of a particular helpee's feelings, each of those feelings will always turn out to have a sufficient reason for the helpee!* One of the most important goals of helpee exploration is to identify—for the helper as well as for the helpee—the helpee's reason for each real feeling.

MEANING RELATES CAUSE AND EFFECT

Remember, feelings are about content. The content provides the reason for the feeling. For example, let us look at several feeling states and related content areas.

Feeling	Content
Happy	about being promoted
Angry	with my teacher for giving me a low grade
Sad	when I knew that I'd never see her again

We may practice responding to meaning by determining the feeling and content of different experiences in our own lives.

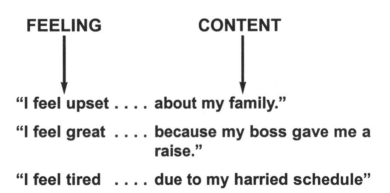

FEELING   CONTENT

"I feel upset . . . . about my family."

"I feel great . . . . because my boss gave me a raise."

"I feel tired . . . . due to my harried schedule"

FEELINGS ARE ABOUT CONTENT

A response to meaning is not complete until it communicates both feeling and content. A response to meaning can be communicated by complementing a response to feeling with a response to content. For example, whereas "You're saying that _____" expressed the content of the helpee's expression and "You feel that _____" expressed the helpee's feelings, "You feel _____ because _____" captures both the feeling and the content. This is an effective format for a complete interchangeable response to the helpee.

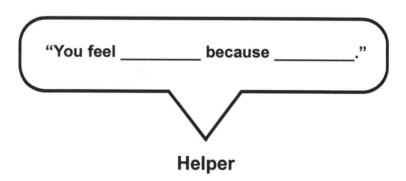

"You feel _____ because _____."

Helper

RESPONDING INTERCHANGEABLY

It is as if we try to understand with our minds what the helpees feel in their guts. We do this by crawling inside of their feelings. Then, we comprehend the reason for the feelings expressed in their content.

Whereas "You feel sad" expresses the helpee's feelings with the passing of a loved one, "You feel sad because she was the most important person in the world to you and now she is gone" captures the meaning of the feeling and the content.

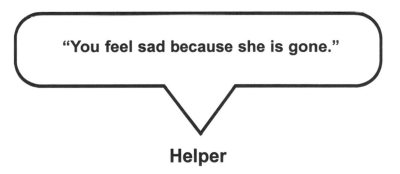

Helper

CAPTURING BOTH THE FEELING AND THE CONTENT

You may feel frustrated because you have been learning to make all responses to meaning in a single format: "You feel _____ because _____." Actually, there are many other ways to communicate a response to meaning. What is critical is that a response to meaning communicates how the helpee feels and the content, or reason, for the feeling. For training purposes, it is recommended that you continue to practice using the "You feel _____ because _____" format. Later, you will formulate and communicate responses to meaning (feeling and content) in your own way.

Here are a few examples of alternative ways to formulate an interchangeable response to meaning:

"You feel _(feeling)_ because _(content)_."
"You feel sad because he moved away."

"You're _(feeling)_ about _(content)_."
"You're sad about his leaving."

"_(Content)_ you feel _(feeling)_."
"Your close friend moved away and now you feel sad."

"Because _(content)_ it's got you feeling _(feeling)_."
"Because he moved away it's got you feeling sad."

"It's _(feeling)_ when _(content)_."
"It's a sad time when a close friend moves away."

**RESPONDING TO MEANING CAN
TAKE MANY FORMS**

The helpees inform us of their readiness to move from exploring where they are in relation to their experiences to understanding where they want or need to be. They alert us by demonstrating their ability to communicate how they feel and the reasons for these feelings. In other words, the helpees inform us of their readiness by doing for themselves the things that we have been doing for them.

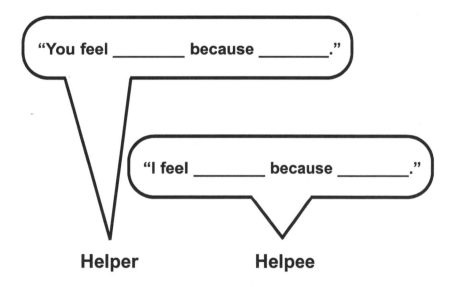

HELPEES SIGNAL THEIR READINESS TO MOVE FROM EXPLORATION TO UNDERSTANDING

Summary

We can measure the accuracy of our responses based on feedback from the helpees. If the helpees continue to explore, then we have been accurate in understanding and communicating what they have said. If we are not accurate in our responses, we cannot help them explore their experiences.

We can measure the comprehensiveness of our responding with the following scale:

High responsiveness — Accurate interchangeable response to meaning (feeling and content)

Moderate responsiveness — Accurate interchangeable response to feeling

Low responsiveness — Accurate interchangeable response to content

Low levels of responsiveness (accurate interchangeable responses to content) are consistent with high levels of attentiveness (listening and repeating verbatim). Moderate levels of responsiveness involve responding to feeling. High levels of responsiveness involve responding to meaning (feeling and content).

LEVELS OF RESPONDING

Now we can continue to build our own cumulative rating scale for helping. If the helper is attentive and accurately responsive to meaning (feeling and content), we can rate the helper at a fully responsive level (level 3.0). If the helper is attentive but accurately responds to feeling alone, we can rate the helper at a partially responsive level (level 2.5). If the helper is attending personally, observing and listening, but accurately responding to only the content of the helpees expressions, we can rate the helper at less than a facilitative level (level 2.0).

LEVELS OF HELPING

5.0
4.5
4.0
3.5
3.0   Responding to meaning
2.5   Responding to feeling
2.0   Responding to content
1.5   Attending personally
1.0   Nonattending

**LEVELS OF HELPING—
ATTENDING AND RESPONDING**

The function of responding to the helpees' experiences is to facilitate their self-exploration of areas of concern. As helpers, we understand that there is no value to exploration unless it facilitates an understanding that goes beyond the material presented. Helpees, however, must first explore where they are in order to understand where they want to be.

When the helpees become able to explore themselves—their feelings, content and meaning—the helpees signal a readiness for the next goal of learning, understanding. This readiness for understanding signals helpers to begin personalizing.

PHASES OF HELPING

PRE-   I

HELPER: Attending Responding

HELPEE: INVOLVING EXPLORING

FACILITATING INVOLVING AND EXPLORING

You now know something about attending and responding skills. You can practice by forming your own responses to the helpee in the following case study. You can also practice by responding to the other case studies in this book and by completing the exercises in the student workbook. Additionally, you can practice with others. You will want to continue practicing these skills until you have integrated them into your helping personality.

Case Study #2—Skilled Responding

Carol Lewis is a thirty-four-year-old woman. She is the mother of three children: four-year-old twin sons, Adam and Aaron, and a six-year-old daughter, Nancy. Carol was widowed when her husband, Mark, died of a malignant brain tumor.

During his last few weeks, Mark was in a hospital. The last four days he was in a coma. Carol stayed at the hospital with him the last five days of his life, leaving the children with her parents.

The Lewis' were assigned to David Biloxi, a hospital social worker. Following is an excerpt of a conversation between David and Carol the day before Mark died. The conversation took place in a private lounge on Mark's ward.

David: "Let's sit down here." (Gestures to the couch). "Would you like some juice or something to eat?"

Carol: (sitting down) "No, I'm not hungry."

David: "You're looking pretty tired."

Carol: "I just haven't been able to sleep much."

David: "This is really a difficult time for you."

Carol: "I'm still not able to believe it's happening. I mean, a month ago we were planning to buy a new house. Mark had just gotten a promotion. And now, any minute he'll be . . . he'll . . . gone."

David: "The whole thing is still unreal. A few weeks ago, the two of you were planning for the future together. Now, Mark is dying."

Carol: "It's so unbelievably unfair!" (shaking her head and clenching her fist)

David: "You're really angry about it all."

Carol: "I'm just so damn mad! Damn mad! God . . . I just don't understand."

David: "You're furious because of the unjustness of Mark's life being cut short."

Carol: "I'm so angry with God and the doctors and everybody."

David: "You're so enraged by what's happening that everyone becomes a target."

Carol: "Yes. And the horrible thing is . . ." (she starts to cry) "I'm so angry with Mark for leaving me. Sometimes I don't know if I can forgive him."

David: "You're especially angry with Mark because he's leaving you, abandoning you."

Carol: (crying harder) "That's right. I just don't know what I'll do without him . . . I love him so much . . . Oh God!"

David: (taking Carol in his arms and holding her as she sobs) "It really hurts seeing him leave you because of how much he means to you."

Carol: "He's been my life . . . even more than the children. With him gone, everything will be so empty. I'll be so . . . alone."

David: "You're frightened because you're going to be alone, having to live without Mark."

Carol: "That's it! That's why I'm so angry. I'm scared of being left alone. How could he do this to me!"

David: "You're frightened because you'll have to start over."

Now look at yourself in your *"mind's eye!"* You will find the clues to your readiness to relate at deeper levels:

- Are you *flying* from the helpees?
- Are you *fighting* with the helpees?
- Are you *relating* to the helpees?

Are you really relating—moving toward them, *"peeling away"* the layers of conditioned facade, discovering their own personal mysteries, generating new directions in their lives. The personal implications of your readiness for this commitment are profound for them—and for you!

RESPONDING ➙ PREPARING FOR PERSONALIZING

6.
PERSONALIZING—FACILITATING UNDERSTANDING

In the practice of helping, personalizing emphasizes *"internalizing"* those experiences that make us *"person-like."* In other words, we become human as we internalize our understanding of ourselves. In short, we *"grow"* ourselves as we "know" ourselves. In this context, personalizing is the heart of helping.

PESONALIZING ➞ GROWTH

Personalizing is the most difficult interpersonal skill to learn and apply. It threatens us because we are put *"on the line."* We feel scared because we cannot change until we have put ourselves *"on the line."* We feel disappointed in ourselves because we cannot personalize our understanding of ourselves or others. We are really eager to learn to personalize. We are hopeful that we can change and grow.

PERSONALIZING ⟶ CHANGE

By responding empathically, we enter the experience of others to help them explore where they are in their lives. By personalizing, we create a dialogue with them that facilitates their understanding where they want to be. It is a dialogue between their *"real"* selves and their *"ideal"* selves. They are unhappy with their *"real"* selves. They are hopeful they can become their *"ideal"* selves. By personalizing this understanding, we are their agents of change.

"REAL" ⟶ "IDEAL"

Born of an empathic and ethical attitude, personalizing is served by a set of skills that enable us to accomplish spiraling levels of understanding through which we

- Become *"one"* with the experience of others
- Process the meaning of this experience
- Process the problems embedded in the meaning
- Generate goals to remediate problems
- Recycle the new experiences as we prepare for acting

In short, personalizing is a developmental process for understanding ourselves, others and the world about us. Personalizing moves us from immaturity to maturity in helping and life. Archimedes said, *"Give me a lever long enough and I will change the world."* Personalizing is that lever!

PERSONALIZING—HIGHLY LEVERAGED SKILLS

Personalizing builds upon the interchangeable base we have established with our responding skills.

We facilitate personalized understanding when we assist the helpees in internalizing, or owning, the meaning of their experiences, their problems or deficits, and their goals or the assets they want and need. Helper personalizing involves the formulation and communication of personalized or individualized responses to meaning, problems and goals.

Personalizing also involves recycling the new feelings that are attendant to the personalized meaning, problems and goals. Personalizing facilitates helpee understanding and prepares us for initiating helpee action.

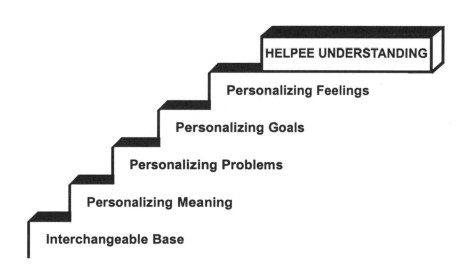

**PERSONALIZING FACILITATES
HELPEE UNDERSTANDING**

Personalizing assists helpees in internalizing their experiences. Often we find that helpees talk about third persons: friends, employers, teachers, spouses, parents, children. By focusing upon others, the helpees *externalize* their experiences. By focusing upon themselves, the helpees *internalize* their experiences.

When responding "interchangeably" to meaning, we used the externalizing format: "You feel (feeling) because (content)." Now we internalize their experiences by introducing the helpees into the responses using the format: "You feel (feeling) because you *(meaning, problem or goal)*."

All personalized responses emphasize "internalizing"— making the helpees accountable for their experiences. We communicate this accountability by including the word *you* after the word *because* in our descriptions of the personalized meaning, problems and goals.

Personalizing Goals
"You feel _____
because **you** cannot (problem)
and **you** want to (goal)."

Personalizing Problems
"You feel _____
because **you** cannot (problem)."

Personalizing Meaning
"You feel _____
because **you** (meaning)."

INTERNALIZING EXPERIENCES WITH PERSONALIZED RESPONSES

Interchangeable Base

To make effective personalized responses, we must first establish a base of communication. When we have made multiple responses that incorporate accurately the content, feeling and meaning expressed by the helpees, we say that we have established an interchangeable base of communication. This interchangeable base provides us with an opportunity to check the accuracy of our understanding of what the helpees have been communicating to us. It also provides an opportunity for the helpees to find out if we are willing and able to understand what they are telling us. We can be "additive" in our communications only after we have first been "interchangeable." The establishment of an interchangeable base of communication is critical to any helping relationship.

INTERCHANGEABLE BASE

**ESTABLISHING AN INTERCHANGEABLE
BASE OF COMMUNICATION**

In building an interchangeable base of communication, the helpees will inform us directly, through their behaviors, of their readiness to move from exploration to understanding. They alert us by demonstrating their ability to sustain self-exploratory behavior. In other words, the helpees inform us of their readiness for movement to the next level by doing for themselves the things that we have been doing for them.

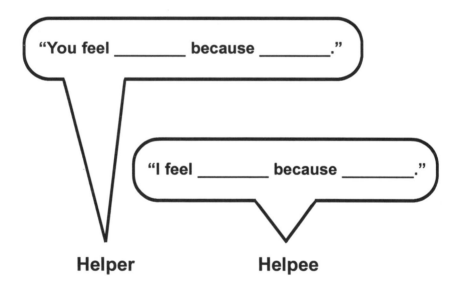

"You feel _____ because _____."

"I feel _____ because _____."

Helper   Helpee

HELPEES SHOW THEIR READINESS TO MOVE FROM EXPLORATION TO UNDERSTANDING

Personalizing Meaning

Personalizing meaning is the first step toward facilitating the helpees' understanding of where they are in relation to where they want or need to be. We personalize the meaning when we "add" to the helpees' understanding of the meaning of their experiences.

In responding "interchangeably" to meaning we answered the questions: "What is the situation?" and "How does the helpee feel about it?" In personalizing meaning we answer the questions: "What are the effects of the situation upon the helpee?" (Implications) and "What personal beliefs cause the helpee to feel this way about the situation?" (Assumptions).

Personalizing meaning involves building on *common* themes to formulate and communicate the *implications* of the helpees' experiences for the helpees. Personalizing meaning also involves formulating and communicating the helpees' *assumptions*. These personal assumptions explain "why" they feel this way.

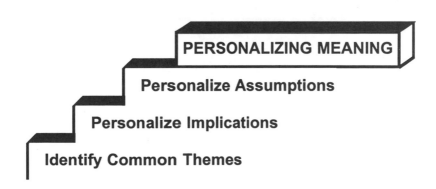

PERSONALIZING MEANING

Just as we formulated interchangeable responses to individual helpee expressions, we now formulate interchangeable responses to helpee expressions made over a period of time. We do this by looking for the common themes in the helpee's expressions. The themes relate to what the helpees are saying about themselves. The common themes are those themes that are interwoven through more than one of the helpee's expressions. When one common theme stands out above others because of recurrence or intensity, we may call it a dominant theme. We now formulate interchangeable responses to the helpee's expressions made over a period of time.

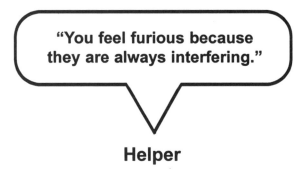

"You feel furious because they are always interfering."

Helper

IDENTIFYING COMMON THEMES

We personalize meaning by considering the personal implications for the helpees. We do this by asking ourselves, "What are the effects of the situation upon the helpees?" We are looking at the personal consequences of their experiences.

We are "additive" when we formulate and communicate information about implications for the helpees that they cannot or will not articulate for themselves. We formulate our personalized responses to meaning by searching our own experiences and our own understanding of implications. We build upon what the helpees' tell and show us, and extend their understanding of the implications of their experiences and their role in it.

When we communicate a personalized response to meaning, we may use the format: "You feel _____ because you _(personal implications)_."

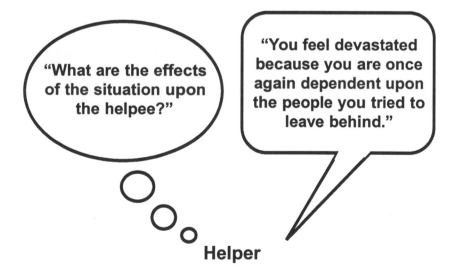

PERSONALIZING IMPLICATIONS

We also personalize meaning when we consider the personal assumptions of the helpee. We do this by asking ourselves, "What personal beliefs cause the helpee to feel this way about the situation?" We are looking for the helpee's personal assumptions about the situation. By "personal assumptions" we mean those beliefs that the helpee holds as accurate or true.

We are "additive" when we formulate and communicate information about the assumptions that the helpees cannot, or will not, articulate for themselves. We formulate our personalized responses to meaning by searching our own experiences and our own understanding of assumptions. We build upon what the helpees tell and show us, and extend their understanding of their personal assumptions about their experiences and their role in it.

In personalizing meaning, we may use the format: "You feel _____ because you _(personal assumptions)_."

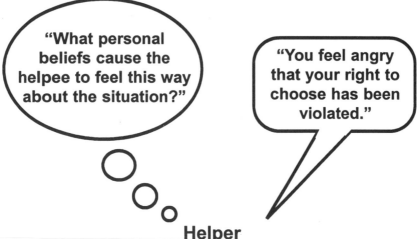

PERSONALIZING ASSUMPTIONS

We must continue to check back with the helpees to stay in tune with their experiences. In so doing, we may find that their feelings are changing. If we do not have a precisely accurate feeling response, we continue to work on answering the feeling question, again asking ourselves, "If I were the helpee, how would I feel?"

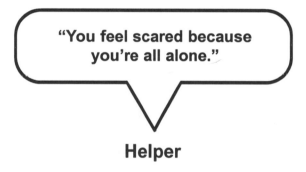

**PERSONALIZING CHANGING FEELINGS
ABOUT MEANING**

The behavioral responses of the helpees will tell us if our personalized responses have been effective. Do the helpees integrate better ideas and better responses? Do the helpees engage in exploring new meanings (assumptions and implications) of their experience?

The helpees inform us of their readiness to move beyond discussing the meaning of their experiences when they demonstrate their ability to formulate and communicate their understanding of the assumptions and the implications of their experiences. In other words, the helpees inform us by doing for themselves the things that we have been doing for them.

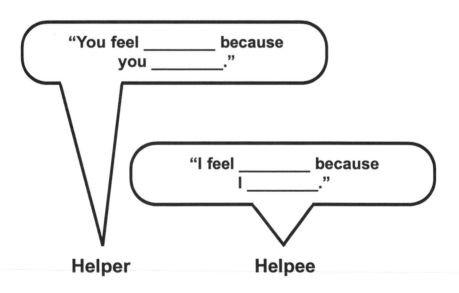

HELPEES SIGNAL THEIR READINESS TO BEGIN UNDERSTANDING PROBLEMS

Personalizing Problems

Personalizing problems is the most critical transitional step to action. It is from defining problems in new ways that we derive new goals. It is from new goals that we derive new action programs.

By personalizing meaning, the helpees have begun to understand their situation in terms of its internal, rather than external, significance. The helpees, however, have still not grappled with their behaviors and how they may be contributing to the situation.

When we personalize problems, we help them to understand what it is that they are unable to do that has led to their present experience of themselves. In other words, we answer the question: "What is there about the helpees themselves that is contributing to the problems?" We are asking the helpees to take responsibility for their lives and to look at themselves as the source of their problems. Personalizing problems involves conceptualizing, internalizing and specifying deficits.

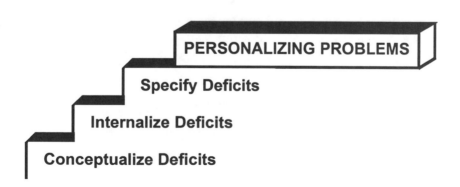

PERSONALIZING PROBLEMS

Specify Deficits

Internalize Deficits

Conceptualize Deficits

PERSONALIZING PROBLEMS

When conceptualizing deficits, we ask these questions of ourselves: "What is missing that is contributing to the problem?" and "What is it that the helpee is failing to do that is contributing most directly to this problem?" We are attempting to ascertain the missing ingredient that might be contributing to the problem. Sometimes we are initially unaware of what that ingredient might be. We must search our own experiences and our own understanding of human health and development. We may have to search out expert information and people for advice.

For example, in a review of physical, emotional and intellectual ingredients for human health and development, we may find the helpees deficit in skills, knowledge or attitude in any of these areas:

- Physical energy
- Motivation
- Interpersonal relating
- Specific information
- Learning
- Thinking or processing

When helpees are unable to conceptualize their own deficits, it is the helper who will conceptualize the helpees' deficits. We may conceptualize the deficit by thinking in terms of the format: " (deficit) is missing."

"Job skills are missing."

Helper

CONCEPTUALIZING DEFICITS

To assist the helpees in internalizing their deficits, we will formulate responses that communicate the helpees' accountability or responsibility for their deficits. Our "additive" personalized responses will assist the helpees to understand their roles in their problems. Our personalized responses will answer the helpee's internalizing question: "What is there about me that is contributing to the problem?"

We may formulate our personalized responses to the problem by thinking in terms of the format: "You feel _____ because you cannot _(problem/deficit)_."

> "You feel hopeless because you cannot manage to get a job."

Helper

INTERNALIZING DEFICITS

Finally, it is important to specify the deficit. If we can specify the deficit, then we will be able to specify the goal and, therefore, make it achievable. The helpee's problem or deficit can be described as a behavior or series of behaviors. Use the format: "You feel _____ because you cannot (problem/deficit) ."

> "You feel disappointed because you cannot present yourself to prospective employers effectively."

Helper

SPECIFYING DEFICITS

We need to stay tuned to the new feelings attendant to the personalized problem. Personalizing feeling emphasizes responding to how the helpees feel about themselves in relation to their deficits. When helpees internalize a deficit, their feelings about themselves and their experiences will often change. We continue to ask the empathy question: "If I were the helpee, how would I feel?" For example, feelings of disappointment—the most common helpee feeling about deficits—may become feelings of weakness or vulnerability because the helpees lack responses to handle their situations.

"You feel vulnerable because your inability to present yourself to prospective employers has left you without a job and without direction."

Helper

PERSONALIZING CHANGING FEELINGS ABOUT DEFICITS

The helpees inform us of their readiness to move from discussing their problems to discussing their goals. They alert us by demonstrating their ability to formulate and communicate their understanding of their problems or deficits. In other words, the helpees inform us by doing for themselves the things that we have been doing for them.

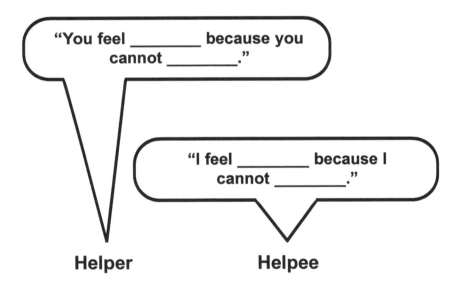

HELPEES SIGNAL THEIR READINESS TO BEGIN UNDERSTANDING GOALS

Personalizing HRD Problems

We may facilitate personalizing problems by the use of the HRD profile illustrated in Table 1 and elaborated in Table 2, Appendix B. As may be viewed, we may assess levels of functioning on our physical, emotional and intellectual resources. We employ a scaling procedure for assessing levels of functioning: leader, contributor, participant, observer, detractor. We also break down the resource components: physical fitness; emotional, motivation and relating; intellectual, information relating, representing and processing. As can be seen, this HRD model enables us to discriminate the current and desired levels of functioning on each of these resource components.

TABLE 1
HUMAN CAPITAL DEVELOPMENT
AREAS AND DIMENSIONS

LEVELS OF FUNCTIONING	PHYSICAL	EMOTIONAL		INTELLECTUAL		
	PHYSICAL FITNESS	PERSONAL MOTIVATION	INTERPERSONAL RELATING	INFORMATIONAL RELATING	INFORMATIONAL REPRESENTING	INTELLECTUAL PROCESSING
5 LEADER						
4 CONTRIBUTOR						
3 PARTICIPANT						
2 OBSERVER						
1 DETRACTOR						

Utilizing the HRD model, we may respond to personalize physical problems at various levels:

"You feel down because you don't have the energy to get through each day."

"You feel disappointed because you cannot mobilize enough intensity to complete your work."

"You feel sad because you just don't have the stamina to stay the course."

"You feel down because you cannot manage your physical requirements."

Helper

PERSONALIZING PHYSICAL PROBLEMS

In a similar manner, we may personalize emotional problems at various levels:

"You feel crushed because you can't get motivated to achieve at high levels."

"You feel desperate because you have not been able to actualize yourself."

"You feel devastated because you can't relate to the experiences of others."

"You feel down because you cannot manage your emotional requirements."

Helper

PERSONALIZING EMOTIONAL PROBLEMS

Likewise, we may use HRD models to personalize intellectual problems at various levels:

"You feel distressed because you can't get the gist of the information."

"You feel disturbed because you don't know how to represent the information."

"You feel hopeless because you can't think about the information productively."

"You feel down because you cannot manage your intellectual requirements."

Helper

PERSONALIZING INTELLECTUAL PROBLEMS

Personalizing Goals

Personalizing goals is the simplest transitional step. If we have personalized the problem effectively, then we should be able to personalize the goal fluidly.

Personalizing goals involves establishing where the helpees want to be in relation to where they are. It involves communicating the helpees' disappointment for some acknowledged responsibility in failing and communicating the helpees' relief and excitement in a direction or solution. The basic way to personalize goals is to determine the behaviors that are the opposite of the personalized problem. Thus, the goal can be described as the "flip side" of the problem. Personalizing goals involves conceptualizing, internalizing and specifying desired or needed assets.

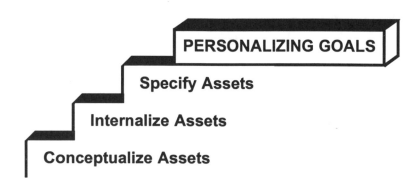

PERSONALIZING GOALS

Just as we conceptualized the deficits, so conceptualize the desired assets. We simply question "What is there about the helpees that to the problem?" by asking, "What might contribute to resolving the problem?" Usually, we can find the desired assets by directly reversing the deficits. Thus, for example, an interpersonal skills problem, or deficit, implies an interpersonal skills goal, or asset. In other words, the goal behavior can be defined as the opposite or "flip side" of the problem behavior. We may conceptualize the needed asset by thinking in terms of the format: "You cannot (problem/deficit) and you want to (goal/asset)."

> "You cannot relate effectively to potential employers and you want to be able to relate effectively with them."

Helper

CONCEPTUALIZING ASSETS

To assist the helpees in internalizing the assets that they need, we will formulate responses that communicate what it is that the helpees will do to solve their problems. Our "additive" personalized responses will assist the helpees to understand their roles in their solutions or goals. Our responses will answer the helpee's internalizing question: "What is it that I will do to contribute to solving the problem?"

When formulating a personalized response that internalizes the desired assets, we may think in terms of the format: "You feel _____ because you cannot _(problem/deficit)_ and you want to _(goal/asset)_ ."

"You feel disappointed because you cannot relate effectively to potential employers and you want to be able to relate effectively with them."

Helper

INTERNALIZING ASSETS

We will want to specify potential desired assets just as we specified deficits. Again, we may need to search out some sources of expertise in specifying these assets. We are beginning to determine which specific assets will be needed to achieve the helpees' goals. Assets are described as a behavior or series of behaviors. When we specify the assets, we are making the goals achievable. In specifying assets, we may use the formula: "You feel _____ because you cannot _(problem/deficit)_ and you want to _(goal/asset)_."

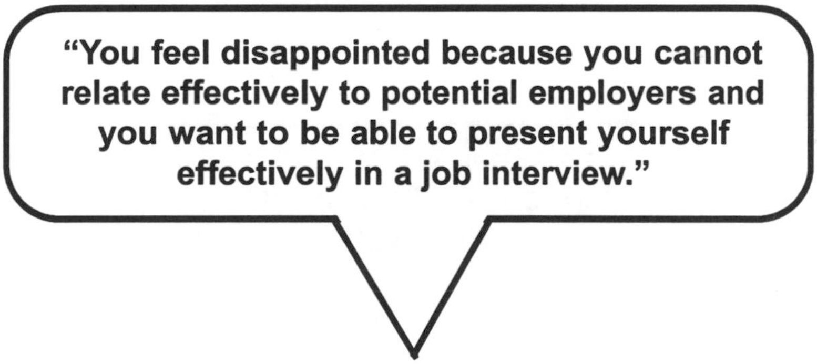

"You feel disappointed because you cannot relate effectively to potential employers and you want to be able to present yourself effectively in a job interview."

Helper

SPECIFYING ASSETS

Just as we personalized changing feelings about deficits or problems, so do we personalize changing feelings about assets or goals. Similarly, just as "down" feelings are usually attached to problems, so are "up" feelings, or feelings of happiness, usually attached to goals. Thus, the helpees usually become hopeful for their futures or pleased with having a direction. We continue to ask the empathy question: "How would I feel if I were the helpee?" In personalizing feelings about goals, we may use the format: "You feel _____ because you are going to _____."

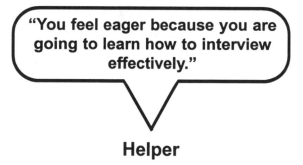

"You feel eager because you are going to learn how to interview effectively."

Helper

**PERSONALIZING CHANGING FEELINGS
ABOUT ASSETS**

The helpees inform us of their readiness to move from understanding to action. They alert us by demonstrating their ability to formulate and communicate their understanding of their goals. In other words, the helpees inform us of their readiness by doing for themselves the things that we have been doing for them.

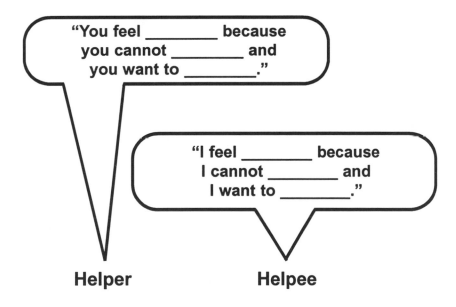

HELPEES SIGNAL THEIR READINESS TO MOVE FROM UNDERSTANDING TO ACTION

Personalizing HRD Goals

In the same manner as personalizing problems, we may personalize goals using the HRD model elaborated in Appendix B. As may be viewed, the diagnosis of the resource deficits leads directly to setting objectives for functioning: detractors seek to become observers; observers to become participants; participants to become contributors; contributors to become leaders in any or all of the resource components.

Using the HRD model, then, we may personalize physical goals at various levels:

"You feel happy to become energized."

"You're looking forward to mobilize to become intensely energized to do your work."

"You're eager to get the stamina along with the intensity in your life."

"You feel up because you are learning to manage your physical requirements."

Helper

PERSONALIZING PHYSICAL GOALS

In a similar manner, we may personalize emotional goals at various levels:

"You feel excited about learning to have pride in craftsmanship."

"You feel elated at the possibility of actualizing yourself."

"You feel overjoyed at learning to relate effectively to others."

"You feel up because you are learning to manage your emotional requirements."

Helper

PERSONALIZING EMOTIONAL GOALS

Likewise, we may use HRD models to personalize intellectual goals at various levels:

"You feel energized by learning to relate to understand information operations."

"You feel wonderful about learning how to represent information operations."

"You feel hopeful that you will learn to think generatively."

"You feel up because you are learning to manage your Intellectual requirements."

Helper

PERSONALIZING INTELLECTUAL GOALS

Personalizing Decision Making

Sometimes we will need to use decision-making strategies to specify goals. These are processes whereby we evaluate courses of action for resolving problems or achieving goals. These decision-making strategies provide a personalized transition into acting. They require us to address the following:

- Problems
- Goals
- Values
- Courses
- Choices

Our helpee, Jane, is having a difficult time juggling work and family responsibilities.

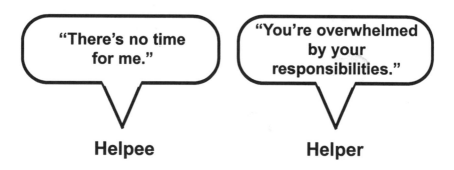

We have already learned the skills of personalizing problems. To use decision-making skills we begin with a problem that we have identified. In our illustration, personal problems are defined as ineffective behaviors that result from skill, knowledge or attitude (S,K,A) deficits. Helpees may not have the critical skills, knowledge or attitudes to manage important areas of their lives.

For example, Jane feels trapped by her many responsibilities and is overwhelmed by a constant barrage of new demands upon her. In this simple example, "time" is identified as a problem area and "life management" is Jane's S,K,A deficit.

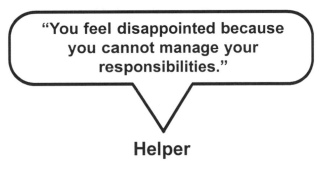

"You feel disappointed because you cannot manage your responsibilities."

Helper

PROBLEM: — S,K,A

PERSONALIZING PROBLEMS

We have also learned the skills of personalizing goals. As we now know, the goals are the flip side of the problems. Where the helpees have deficits in skills, knowledge or attitudes (S,K,A), they may generate goals for developing skills, knowledge or attitude assets.

To continue the illustration, for Jane, "time" is identified as the goal area and some kind of "life management" may be the S,K,A she wants and needs to master.

> "You feel disappointed because you cannot manage your responsibilities and you want to be able to handle them more effectively."

Helper

PROBLEM: — S,K,A
GOALS: + S,K,A

PERSONALIZING GOALS

Next we may generate alternative courses of action for achieving our goals. One helpful way of developing alternatives is to expand people alternatives ("Who else might become involved?"), program alternatives ("What else might be done?") and organization options ("How might we reconfigure people and program resources?").

For example, Jane may consider people courses of action, such as getting a babysitter or a housekeeper; program courses of action, such as studying time management at the Community College or at the counseling center; or, organizational courses of action, such as quitting her job or renegotiating her job requirements with her employer.

"You feel hopeful because we are discussing several strategies that might help you reach your goal."

Helper

PROBLEM: — S,K,A
GOALS: + S,K,A

COURSES OF ACTION
People   Programs   Organizations

PERSONALIZING COURSES

We may personalize values for discriminating among alternatives. We have already personalized meaning. Values are the meanings we attach to people, data and things. Values are who and what matters to us. One helpful way of describing values is to describe the living, learning and working benefits we hope to attain. The benefits that we desire guide the efforts we make in life.

For example, Jane may seek the living benefit of having more time to spend with her family, or the learning benefit of having time to study a topic of interest, or the working benefit of having more time to get ahead in her career, or all of the above. And more!

"You're pleased that this decision-making process involves exploring your values."

Helper

PROBLEM: — S,K,A
GOALS: + S,K,A

                    COURSES OF ACTION
VALUES: People   Programs   Organizations

Working
Learning
Living

PERSONALIZING VALUES

Finally, we simply use our values to evaluate our courses of action. This means evaluating how each course impacts each value. One helpful way of evaluating courses is to assign them plus (+), minus (−) or neutral (0) signs according to their impact upon values. After making this evaluation, we can calculate the best alternative(s).

For example, Jane may find that hiring a housekeeper and getting time management training are both preferred courses of action.

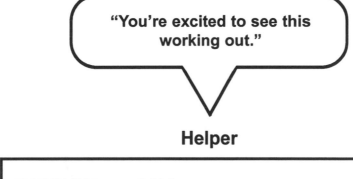

Helper

PROBLEM: — S,K,A
GOALS: + S,K,A

	COURSES OF ACTION		
VALUES:	**People**	**Programs**	**Organizations**
Working	+	+	+
Learning	+	+	−
Living	+	+	−

PERSONALIZING CHOICES

We must emphasize personalizing as a continuing experience. We create an interchangeable base of responsiveness so that we can add to the helpee's understanding. We will recycle our responsiveness until we can personalize a new level of understanding.

Personalized decision making simply provides us with a concrete direction at a point in time. As our human condition changes, our problems, goals, courses, values and choices change. Immaturity is seeing your life as a *"still photo."* Maturity is seeing your life as a *"motion picture."* Personalizing is what puts us in motion!

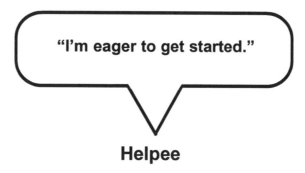

"I'm eager to get started."

Helpee

PERSONALIZING CHANGES

Summary

We can test the comprehensiveness and accuracy of our personalized responses to the helpees' expressions. We begin by simply attending and responding interchangeably. Then we offer personalized responses. We can rate the comprehensiveness and accuracy of our personalizing the helpees' experiences as follows:

High personalizing — Accurately personalized problems, goals and feelings incorporating helpees' response deficits and assets

Moderate personalizing— Accurately personalized meaning incorporating personal assumptions and implications of experience

Low personalizing — Accurate responsiveness to meaning

As can be seen, the low levels of personalizing are consistent with the high levels of responsiveness (feeling and content). The moderate levels of personalizing involve meaning, while the high levels involve the problems, goals and feelings.

LEVELS OF PERSONALIZING

We continue to build our cumulative scale for helping. If the helper is attending, responding and personalizing the meaning, problem, goal and feelings for the helpee, we can rate the helper at a fully personalizing level (level 4.0). If the helper is attentive and responsive and personalizes the meaning for the helpee, we can rate the helper at a facilitatively personalizing level (level 3.5).

LEVELS OF HELPING

5.0
4.5
4.0 Personalizing problem, goal and feeling
3.5 Personalizing meaning
3.0 Responding to meaning
2.5 Responding to feeling
2.0 Responding to content
1.5 Attending
1.0 Nonattending

LEVELS OF HELPING—ATTENDING, RESPONDING AND PERSONALIZING

As we move to personalized levels of responding, we are, as we have seen, introducing our own experience. That is, we are going beyond what the helpees have expressed. We must draw from our own experience, our knowledge of assets and deficits, and our understanding of the helpee.

We can practice personalizing by practicing some of the exercises in the student workbook or by forming responses to the case studies in this book. The best practice, however, will come from working with our classmates and associates. Practice personalizing less intense helpee experiences before attempting to use these skills in intense helping situations.

The keys to formulating effective personalized responses are empathy and discipline. This empathy means being willing and able to see experiences from the perspectives of others. This discipline includes building an interchangeable base, using that base to search out the common or dominant themes, and personalizing meaning, problems, goals and changing feelings. The effectiveness of our formulations may be determined by how well the helpees utilize our personalized attempts.

PHASES OF HELPING

	PRE-	I	II
HELPER:	Attending	Responding	Personalizing
HELPEE:	INVOLVING	EXPLORING	UNDERSTANDING

FACILITATING INVOLVING, EXPLORING AND UNDERSTANDING

You now know about attending, responding and personalizing skills. You will need to work most intensely on your personalizing skills because they are the most difficult to learn. Practice until you can formulate and communicate these responses easily, as the helper does in the following case study.

Case Study #3—Skilled Personalizing

Barbara is a twenty-five-year-old graduate student who will complete her master's degree in physics next semester. However, in the last few months she has become unsure of her desire to be a physicist. She already has several job offers for when she graduates, but has deferred making a decision.

She has sought help from Debbie, a former roommate and friend who is now working in the university's placement office. The following excerpt takes place after two previous sessions and well into the third session.

Barb: "When I realized that the reason I went on with school was to prove to my family that I could do it, I also realized that being a physicist might not be what I really want to do."

Debbie: "You went on to get your master's to prove yourself to your family and now you're not sure if that's what you really want to do."

Barb: "I get so upset with the way they discount me because I'm a woman. They always put my brothers first."

Debbie: "You feel angry because they have never accepted you as an equal to your brothers."

Barb: "The entire thing is just so stupid! I keep trying to prove to them that I'm worthy, and no matter what I do they'll never accept me."

Debbie: "You feel disgusted because they can't recognize what you can do."

Barb: "Yes, but why can't I be satisfied with me knowing what I can do?"

Debbie: "You're angry because you haven't been able to break free from wanting to earn their approval."

Barb: "That's right! I can't be satisfied with myself or what I do because I want their respect."

Debbie: "You feel disgusted with yourself because you have let your need for their respect determine what you do with you life."

Barb: "And now at twenty-five, three months away from a master's in physics, I'm not sure if I really want to be physicist or if I'm doing it solely to earn their love."

Debbie: "You feel scared because you can't be sure that becoming a physicist is something you really want to do for yourself or something you're doing to earn your family's love."

Barb: "I need to find out if I've made a big mistake."

Debbie: "You're unsure about what your own career needs are.

Barb: "Yeah. I'm not even sure how to make such an important decision myself."

Debbie: "You feel discouraged because you can't assert your own needs as indicated by your inability to make a decision."

Barb: "That's a pretty pathetic description of someone about to get her master's, but I guess it's accurate. I just kept doing what I thought my folks wanted, and now here I am . . ."

Debbie: "You're embarrassed by your inability to assert yourself and live your own life."

Barb: "Right. And I think it's about time I do something about that."

Debbie: "You're disappointed in yourself because you don't know how to make decisions and you want to learn to do so."

Barb: "Exactly! When I know how to make my own decisions then I'll know if I'm living my own life or just trying to prove something to my parents."

Debbie: "Now you're energized by the thought of taking control of your life. You want to learn to assert your own needs as indicated by knowing and acting upon the skills of decision making."

More than anything else, then, personalizing is a way of life, a way of growth. We grow when we personalize our experiences in life. We help others to grow when we help them to personalize their experiences. Like any other way of life, you either live it fully or you fail. You cannot fake it! The quality of the study and practice that you give to personalizing will determine whether you grow and become a *"whole"* person; moreover, it will determine whether you can help others to grow and become *"whole."* For personalizing is, indeed, a qualitative dimension! Below level 3, we can learn to attend and respond in quantitative terms. Above level 3, we learn to personalize in qualitative terms. The quality of our lives is determined by the quality of our personalizing.

PERSONALIZING—A WAY OF LIFE

7.
INITIATING—FACILITATING
ACTING

There is no understanding without acting! Simply stated, life is a continuous learning process. The source of this learning is feedback from the environment. Most frequently, we see helpees who have received negative feedback from their environments: they are not living, learning or working effectively. We work with them in helping: exploring their experiences and understanding their goals. If they do not act upon their understanding, they have terminated the learning process and attenuated their growth. Moreover, if we do not initiate to facilitate their acting, the helpees take our behavior as the model for their lives—lives of inaction and deterioration!

NON-INITIATING ⟶ INACTION

Helping initiates a life-long learning process. The feedback from acting is the source of continuous stimulation of that learning process. The helper initiative, which facilitates acting, is central to the effectiveness of acting. Just as the personalized understanding defined new goals, personalized initiatives achieve these goals. Again, the entire helping process is developmental and cumulative, with each phase building upon the skills of the previous phase. When we initiate as helpers, the helpees assume our behavior as the model for their lives—lives of acting and growing!

INITIATING ⟶ ACTING

At the most basic level, acting means behaving in some overt way. It is not enough to develop a plan. We must implement the plan behaviorally in order to impact our environments. It is as if the helper is working with the helpee to test hypotheses in the helpee's life. The impact issue is this: together, can they *"load up"* the independent or intervening variables in such powerful ways as to impact the dependent variables in the helpee's world. In other words, can they *"stack the cards"* to enable the helpee to be successful.

ACTING ⟶ IMPACTING

One way to impact the helpee's world is to enable the helpee to manage that world. We call this *empowering.* Basically, we pass on our own *"powers"* to the helpees. Usually, these *"powers"* are in the form of the skills, knowledge and attitudes that we impart to them. We call this *psychological education or training as treatment.* We *"empower"* the helpees to impact their environments in productive ways. Thus, we break the cycle of negativity and introduce the cycle of productivity.

IMPACTING → PRODUCTIVITY

Initiating is the culminating phase of helping. Initiating emphasizes facilitating the helpees' efforts to act to achieve their goals. In other words, the helpees act to change or gain in their functioning. This action is based upon their personalized understanding of their goals. It is facilitated by the helper's initiative.

Initiating involves defining goals, developing programs, and designing schedules and reinforcements. Initiating also includes preparing to implement steps and planning check steps.

Defining the goals emphasizes the operations that describe the goals. Developing programs emphasizes determining the steps needed to achieve the goals and insuring that the steps are related to the helpee's frame of reference. Designing schedules emphasizes attaching time to steps while designing reinforcements emphasizes attaching reinforcements to steps. Preparing to implement the steps involves reviewing, rehearsing and revising. Then the helpees will check their progress by using "before, during and after check steps."

INITIATING

Plan Check Steps

Prepare to Implement Steps

Design Schedule & Reinforcements

Develop Programs

Define Goals

INITIATING FACILITATES HELPEE ACTING

Defining Goals

The first task in initiating is defining the goal. If we can define the goal, then our direction is clear.

In defining the goal, we need to establish all of the ingredients necessary to achieve the goal. We accomplish this by defining the "5WH information" about the goal and by defining a standard to measure the basic question of direction: "How will we know when we have reached our goal?"

DEFINING GOALS

We need to determine all of the ingredients of our goals. It is important to include all of the people and things that may impinge upon the helpee's achievement of the goals. We need to determine, "Who and what is involved?"

We need to define all of the activities involved. "What will be done?" That way no critical activity is omitted in our attempts to achieve our goals.

It is also important to describe the reasons for accomplishing the goals and the methods to accomplish them. "Why and how will the goals be accomplished?"

We also need to describe when and where the activity will occur. It is important to be specific to insure that the helpee knows when and where the new behavior will take place.

Who and **what** is involved?
What will be done?
How and **why** will the goals be accomplished?
When and **where** will the activities occur?

Helper

DEFINE 5WH OF BEHAVIOR

In order to determine when the helpee has reached the goal, we will need to define observable and measurable standards. Defining standards usually means describing the goal in terms of the number of times or amount of time the helpee is engaged in some behavior. We can define the standard by answering the question: "How well will it be done?"

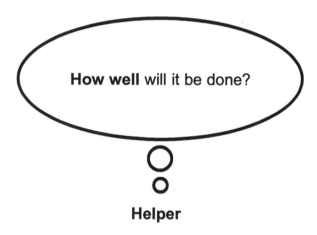

DEFINE STANDARDS

We must now communicate our definition of the goal to the helpee. We do this by emphasizing the behavior and the standards of performance.

We may use the format:

"You want to _____ (5WH of behavior) as indicated by _____ (standards)."

"You want to relate effectively by building an interchangeable base with your parents as indicated by six interchangeable responses at home during mealtimes."

Helpee

COMMUNICATING THE OPERATIONAL GOAL

Developing Programs

In order to achieve the goals, we need to develop programs. Programs are simply step-by-step procedures for achieving the goals. Every step in the program should lead to accomplishing the goal.

Most programs are sequenced by contingency, i.e., each step is dependent upon the performance of the previous step. We determine what steps we must perform as preconditions for the next step. In this context, an action program consists of a well-defined goal, a basic first step, and intermediary and sub-steps, with each step being individualized for the helpee.

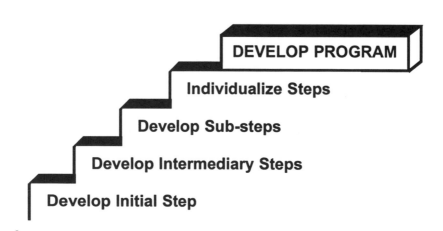

DEVELOP PROGRAM

Individualize Steps

Develop Sub-steps

Develop Intermediary Steps

Develop Initial Step

DEVELOPING PROGRAMS

The first step is the most basic step that the helpee must take. It should be the most fundamental building block in the program. This way we can build the other steps upon it. For example, if the goal is running a mile in eight minutes, the first step might be walking around the block. For some people, the first step to running a mile may be literally taking a first step.

For example: Bill feels disappointed because he cannot relate effectively with his parents and he really wants to learn how to relate effectively. For Bill, the first step in relating to his parents might be attending to them. In communicating the first step, we use a simple, straightforward format.

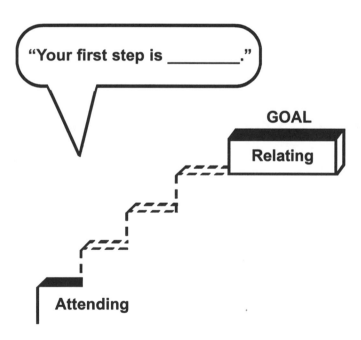

DEVELOPING INITIAL STEPS

Intermediary steps bridge the gap between the first step and the goal. We may determine an intermediary step that is approximately halfway between the first step and the goal. We may then continue our program development by filling in additional intermediary steps. For example, if the goal is running a mile in eight minutes, the intermediary steps might be running from one-quarter, to one-half, to three-quarters, to one mile and from twelve- to ten- to nine- to eight-minute miles

For our helpee, in learning to relate to his parents, the intermediary steps beyond attending might emphasize observing, listening and responding skills. In communicating the intermediary steps, we may use a direct, simple format.

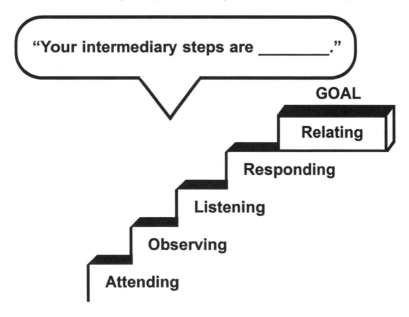

"Your intermediary steps are _____."

GOAL

Relating

Responding

Listening

Observing

Attending

DEVELOPING INTERMEDIARY STEPS

We continue to fill out our program by developing sub-steps. We develop sub-steps by treating each step in the program as a sub-goal and developing the initial and intermediary steps to achieving that sub-goal. We continue to do this until we have all the steps and sub-steps needed to achieve our goal. If we leave out a step or sub-step, our helpees will fail to achieve their goals. If we are planning to run a mile, we must develop distance and time sub-steps.

With our helpee, the steps to the goal of "relating" can be treated as sub-goals, and sub-steps can be developed to achieve these sub-goals just as we have in this book. In communicating the sub-steps, we use a simple format.

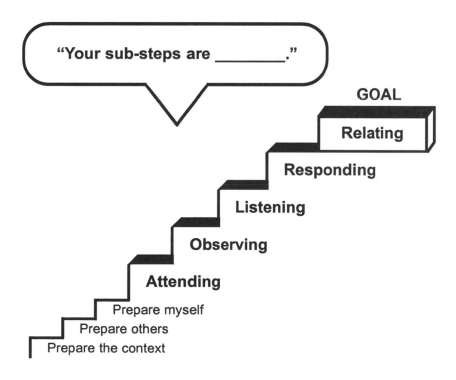

DEVELOPING SUB-STEPS

Some helpees cannot perform the steps as readily as others. They require programs individualized to their own particular learning or processing styles. This is essential as most programs are comprised of steps that are sequenced by contingency, where each step is dependent upon the performance of the previous step.

Every step of initiating should be individualized by checking back with the helpee. We check back with the helpee by making interchangeable responses that insure that we are in tune with the helpee's frame of reference. Even when we individualize the sequencing of steps, we must stay finely tuned because this is a very subtle human process.

INDIVIDUALIZING STEPS

Developing Schedules

The process of initiating continues as we develop time schedules for step and goal achievement. Schedules serve to focus our programs.

The major emphasis in scheduling is on developing starting times and finishing, or completion, times. They tell both helpers and helpees when things are to be done. Starting and finishing times may also be set for individual steps as well as for the overall program. No program is complete without starting times and completion times.

DEVELOP SCHEDULES

Determine Completion Times

Determine Starting Times

DEVELOPING SCHEDULES

The first step in developing schedules is setting specific starting times or dates. For example, we might start walking immediately to achieve our goal of running a mile in eight minutes. With our helpee, we may set a starting time for the interpersonal skills program. In communicating starting times, we may use a simple and direct format.

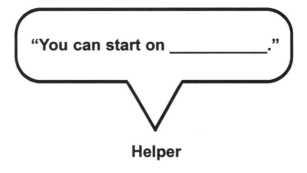

Helper

SETTING STARTING TIMES

The next step in developing schedules is setting specific completion times or dates. For example, we might set a completion time of six months for achieving our goal of running a mile in eight minutes.

In our illustration, our helpee may aim to complete the "relating" program by the end of month two. In communicating completion times, we may use a simple format.

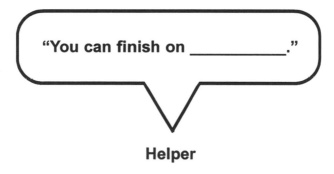

SETTING COMPLETION TIMES

In a similar manner, we can set starting and completion times for each interim step. For example, our helpee might decide that he would spend the next month learning and practicing how to make accurate interchangeable responses. The first week he could concentrate upon attending, observing and listening; the second week upon responding to content; the third week upon responding to feeling; and the fourth week upon responding to feeling, content and meaning. A detailed schedule allows both helpee and helper to monitor the timeliness of the helpee's performance of steps.

"You can start on _____ and finish on _____."

Helper

MONITORING TIMELINESS

Developing Reinforcements

The next step in initiating involves developing reinforcements that will encourage the helpees to take the needed steps. Reinforcements are simply things that matter to us. They are most effective when they are applied immediately following the performance of a step.

The consequences of carrying out the steps to achieve goals and overcome deficits are often too distant for the helpees. More immediate reinforcements must be introduced.

Clearly, these reinforcements must come from the helpee's frame of reference. What we think matters for the helpees must really matter to them. Many helping programs have failed because of their inability to attach appropriate reinforcements. In this context, we continue to emphasize our responsiveness: empathy is the source of all knowledge about powerful reinforcements for the helpees. Sometimes, it may be appropriate for helpees to work with support persons or support groups to monitor their performance and to administer the reinforcements.

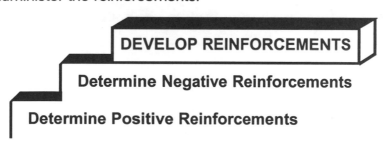

DEVELOP REINFORCEMENTS

Determine Negative Reinforcements

Determine Positive Reinforcements

DEVELOPING REINFORCEMENTS

Positive reinforcements or rewards are our most potent reinforcements. People tend to work hard for things that really matter to them. This means the helper must work diligently to develop the positive reinforcements from the helpee's frame of reference. In turn, the helpee must work diligently to receive the reinforcements.

Our helpee, for example, might decide simply that he would go out with his friends on Friday and Saturday nights as he successfully completed each step of his program. We can develop similar reinforcements for any program. The reinforcements will vary as widely as human nature itself.

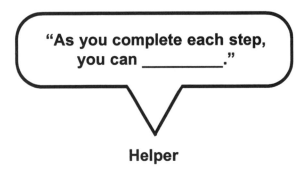

Helper

REINFORCING POSITIVELY

To the degree we can, we want to avoid employing negative reinforcements. We use the term in a restricted sense to mean punishments. In this context, the application of negative reinforcements stimulates other reactions, such as aversive reactions to the person who administers the punishment. Initially, we should attempt to define the negative reinforcements as the absence of rewards.

In our helpee's case, he defined his own negative reinforcements as the absence of rewards. Specifically, he decided to stay home on the weekend to work on the uncompleted step in his program. Again, similar negative reinforcements may be designed and applied in other programs. Like rewards, negative reinforcements vary widely, and to use them effectively, we must be finely tuned to the people involved.

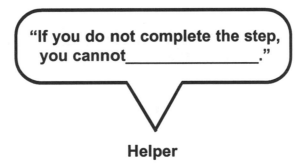

"If you do not complete the step, you cannot_____."

Helper

REINFORCING NEGATIVELY

If it is unclear whether a step was performed in a satisfactory manner, then we must vigilantly observe the performers. We do so to determine whether the helpees are moving toward or away from the goals. Ultimately, all behavior is either goal-directed or not goal-directed.

Once we come to understand the helpees' behaviors we respond to positively reinforce the goal-directed behavior of our helpees and to negatively reinforce the negative, goalless behavior. We are aligning ourselves with what is healthy in the individuals and opposing that which is unhealthy. We communicate our respect for them as people, but not for their unhealthy behavior. We may use ourselves as potent reinforcers by being conditional. We can do this by spelling out the implications of the helpee's behavior for our own behavior.

> **"If you do (not) say/feel/do _____,
> then I will (not) say/feel/do _____."**

Helper

**OBSERVING VIGILANTLY AND
REINFORCING CONDITIONALLY**

Preparing to Implement Steps

The final steps of preparation before implementation emphasize reviewing, rehearsing and revising the steps of the program. Reviewing insures the inclusiveness of our steps. Rehearsing helps us find the problems involved in implementing the steps. Revising emphasizes the final changes in the program. These steps prepare us for the implementation of the program and are necessary if we wish to succeed.

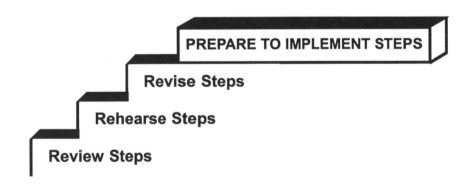

PREPARE TO IMPLEMENT STEPS

Revise Steps

Rehearse Steps

Review Steps

PREPARING TO IMPLEMENT STEPS

We must review the definitions of our goals, the steps of the program, schedules and the consequences or reinforcement of behavior. For example, in our running program, we must check all distances and time steps.

In implementing the interpersonal relating program, our helpee must begin by reviewing all steps and sub-steps of attending personally, observing, listening and responding. Reviewing gives us a chance to make sure that we have included all necessary steps in the program.

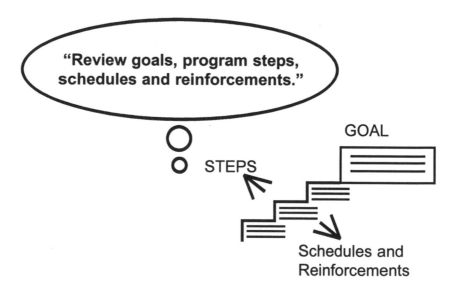

REVIEWING STEPS

By rehearsing all the steps of the program, we get a chance to pilot our final performance. Rehearsing gives us the opportunity to find the problems involved in the final implementation of the steps. For example, in our running program, we can try ourselves out in real-life running situations.

In implementing the interpersonal relating program, our helpee may rehearse all of the attending and responding steps. Again, rehearsal is necessary if we care about being successful.

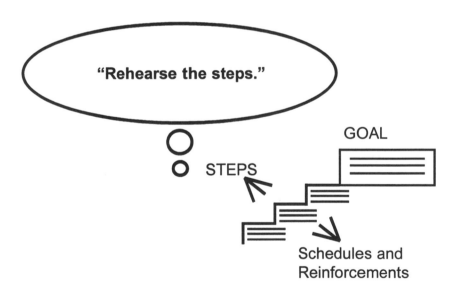

REHEARSING STEPS

The purpose of reviewing and rehearsing is revising. We now incorporate all of the necessary revisions in the steps of the program. We will revise the program again when we get feedback from our action step. In our running program, we may revise our time and distance estimates upward or downward.

In implementing the interpersonal attending program, our helpee may revise some of the steps or sub-steps in order to increase the effectiveness of his action. Revising insures our probability of succeeding.

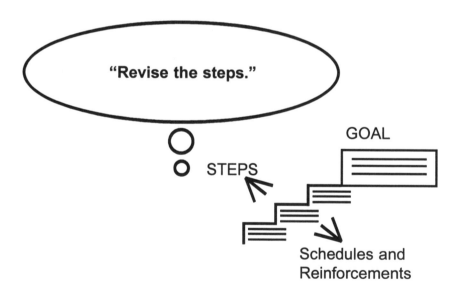

REVISING STEPS

Planning Check Steps

One of the ways of ensuring success is to develop check steps. Check steps emphasize the things we need to think about before, during and after the performance of each program step. They emphasize the resources we need to be successful and the ways to monitor and assess our effectiveness in performing the steps.

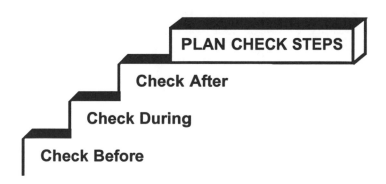

PLANNING CHECK STEPS

The "before check steps" emphasize the things we need to do before we perform each step. They ask and answer the question: "What resources will I need to perform the step successfully?" These resources include physical, emotional and intellectual resources. For example, in planning to run a mile, physically we need a measured distance and stopwatch as well as some appropriate kind of running shoes and clothes. Emotionally we need motivation for achieving our goal, and intellectually we need a step-by-step program.

In implementing the interpersonal attending steps of the relating program, our helpee needs an appropriate physical setting and an occasion to interact with people, such as that provided by mealtime in his home. In addition, he needs an emotional commitment and an intellectual program to achieve his goal. Without the resources, we are unable to perform the steps effectively. The "before check steps" give us an opportunity to check out our resources before performing the steps.

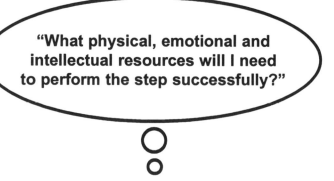

BEFORE CHECK STEPS

"During check steps" emphasize the things we need to do during the performance of each step. These check steps ask and answer the question "Am I performing the step correctly?" Again, this involves physical, emotional and intellectual dimensions. Physically, in running, we may check our times and distances. Emotionally, we may check out our level of motivation. Intellectually, we may check whether we are running with proper form or appropriate breathing.

In implementing the interpersonal relating program, our helpee may check physically whether he is squared with others, sitting forward at a 200 angle and making eye contact. Emotionally, he may check whether he is being fully attentive to others. Intellectually, he may check whether he is focused on the content and feeling of the others' expressions. The "during check steps" give us an opportunity to check ourselves out during the performance of the steps.

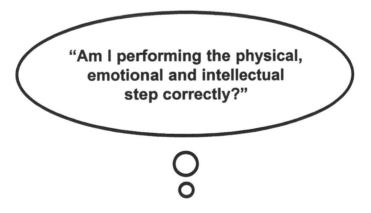

DURING CHECK STEPS

"After check steps" emphasize the things we need to do after the performance of each step. We ask and answer the question: "Did I achieve the results and benefits I wanted?" These are physical, emotional and intellectual results and benefits. For example, in implementing the running program we might check to see if we ran the intended distance within the targeted time and gained the physical and emotional benefits. Intellectually, we may check any earnings gained from the achievement of the program step.

In implementing the interpersonal attending program, our helpee may check out whether he did or did not attend effectively. He may also check whether his attentiveness facilitated his parents' involvement in a conversation with him. He may check whether the conversation led to the desired benefits of improved relations.

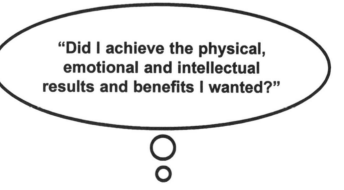

"Did I achieve the physical, emotional and intellectual results and benefits I wanted?"

`AFTER CHECK STEPS

Summary

We can test the comprehensiveness of our initiative responses to the helpees' experience by rating our initiative responses to the helpees as follows:

High initiative — Implementing steps

Moderate initiative — Defining goals and developing programs

Low initiative — Personalizing goals

As can be seen, the low levels of initiative are consistent with the high levels of personalizing (goal). The moderate levels of initiative involve defining goals and developing programs while the high levels involve implementing steps.

LEVELS OF INITIATIVE

We can now complete our cumulative scale for helping. If the helper is attending, responding, personalizing and initiating to develop the steps to achieve the operationally defined goal, then the helper is operating at a fully initiative level (level 5.0). If the helper is initiating only to define the goal, then the helper can be rated at an initiative level (level 4.5).

LEVELS OF HELPING

5.0	Initiating steps
4.5	Defining goals
4.0	Personalizing problem, goal and feeling
3.5	Personalizing meaning
3.0	Responding to meaning
2.5	Responding to feeling
2.0	Responding to content
1.5	Attending
1.0	Nonattending

LEVELS OF HELPING—ATTENDING, RESPONDING, PERSONALIZING AND INITIATING

Developing initiative is the culminating act in the helping process. Given personalized goals, initiating enables us to define operational goals and to develop programs to achieve the goals. Resolving the helpees' problems and achieving their goals is what helping is all about.

We must constantly check back with the helpee's frame of reference during the process of initiating. We do this by making accurate responses to the helpee's experiences. At the highest levels of helping, responding and initiating are integrally related. There is no true responsiveness that does not result in action. There is no accurate action that is not built on responsiveness.

PHASES OF HELPING

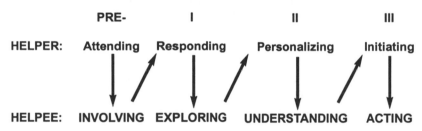

FACILITATING INVOLVING, EXPLORING, UNDERSTANDING AND ACTING

You now know something about the basic helping skills: attending, responding, personalizing and initiating. You will need to work in a most intense and disciplined manner to master these skills. Practice until you can formulate and communicate these responses fluidly and effectively as part of your own helping personality. You might begin by making your own responses to the helpees in the following case study.

Case Study #4—Skilled Initiating

In a group of substance abusers are three men and one woman. Zeke is a nineteen-year-old college dropout who referred himself to treatment after an overdose of alcohol and tranquilizers that almost killed him. Frank is a twenty-five-year-old who is in treatment as a condition of his probation for grand larceny. His drug of choice was cocaine. Mandy is a seventeen-year-old chronic runaway who was referred to treatment by her parents after her last run. She has been a multiple-drug user. Mitch is a twenty-two-year-old college student who was referred to treatment by a friend. He stated he was having problems with "pot" and alcohol.

Lois, the helper, is a woman in her mid-thirties. She has been a substance abuse counselor for the last five years. She has never had a problem with drugs or alcohol herself.

The room is set up with chairs and a chart pad in a circle. The room is bright and cheery. There are no anti-drug or alcohol posters on the walls. There are several very good, dramatic watercolor portraits of people expressing intense emotions.

(This is an excerpt from the third counselling session. It starts about ten minutes into the session.)

Mandy: "Frank, you're looking irritated, with that scowl on your face."

Zeke: "Yeah, what's bothering you?"

Lois: "It sounds like some of the others have noticed it too, Frank."

Frank: "It's not anything I really want to talk about."

Mandy: "Okay, it's hard to open up, but that's one of the reasons why we're here; because we don't really communicate."

Frank: "Listen you little _____, when I want your advice I'll ask for it!"

Lois: "You're really torn up by what's bothering you. You're so angry you're lashing out at anyone."

Frank: "Hey, Mandy, I'm sorry . . . I just . . . I don't know."

Mandy: "Listen, I've been called worse. It's okay."

Lois: "You feel frightened because you aren't sure what we might say or do if you tell us what's concerning you."

Frank: "It's not that I don't trust you . . . It's just personal."

Zeke: "It's really hard to start opening up to people you hardly know."

Lois: "Frank, you're struggling with something that's really overwhelming and you don't want to lose control."

Frank: (silence, looking at the floor, trembling noticeably) "Yeah."

Lois: (gets up from her chair, squats down in front of Frank, and takes his hands) "You're in so much pain that you can hardly stand it." (Frank bursts into tears and hugs Lois. Mandy and Zeke, who are sitting next to Frank, each put a hand on his shoulder. Mitch sits watching, looking uncomfortable. After about a minute Frank starts to calm down. Lois hands him a tissue.)

Frank: "I'm sorry. I've never done anything like that before . . . it's just . . ." (he blows his nose) "it hurts so bad."

Mandy: "So tell us what has you so torn to pieces."

Frank: "I've been dating this girl and I really like her. I thought we had something special going. Things were going fine, but then someone told her about my drug use and my record. "Now, she doesn't want to see me again. She said that I had lied to her, that I didn't tell her the truth about myself. I wanted to tell her about what I've been through; I just didn't know how."

Zeke: "Wow!"

Lois: "You're really devastated by your girlfriend confronting you and leaving you."

Frank: "Yeah, it really hurts. But the tough part is that I really have a difficult time meeting people. She was just about the only person outside this room I could talk to who isn't into drugs."

Mandy: "Yeah, I know what you mean. I don't have anyone either. I tried a couple of times, but no one wanted to have anything to do with me."

Lois: "Frank, you feel really frightened because of how lonely the world is for you. And Mandy, you sound really angry because you've tried to reach out and have been rejected."

Mandy: "At least when I was into partying I wasn't so lonely."

Lois: "You feel humiliated because you think straight kids won't have anything to do with you."

Mandy: "Yeah, they all think I'm strange. They won't have anything to do with me. I mean, at least when I did drugs I could shut off all this stuff. At least then I had friends."

Lois: "You're frightened because you don't think you'll be able to relate to another person without drugs."

Mandy: "I've messed up my life so bad I can't believe that anyone could like me. I mean, I've abused myself. Who'd want me now?"

Lois: "You're terrified because you don't believe you'll find any other way to be wanted."

Mandy: (tears on her cheeks) "I guess I'm not as tough as I thought."

Mitch: "Mandy?" (She looks up. He reaches over to her hesitantly.) "I don't really know how to say this, but I think you're being too tough on yourself." (Mandy makes a hesitant smile.)

Lois: "You seem to be having the same feeling of hurt and fear of being alone, Mitch."

Mitch: (hesitantly) "Yeah, well..."

Zeke: "I sure can relate to what she's saying. I mean, I look back on my life and I'm so . . . ashamed! I just can't believe I can be any different. Who'd want to know a sleaze ball like me, you know?"

Lois: "You feel ashamed and disgusted, too. You don't know how to start fresh with people." (turning back to Mitch) "But, Mitch, I was hearing more pain, more yearning, in your voice, rather than shame or disgust."

Mitch: "Yeah, I've been lonely and scared of people. I guess that's why I drank and smoked dope. It helped me feel powerful and in control, you know."

Lois: "So you feel frightened because you don't know how to relate to people either."

Mitch: "That's right."

Lois: "Frank, you feel hurt because you don't know if you can find someone to relate with. Mandy, you're scared that you'll never be able to experience real intimacy with someone. Mitch, you're frightened because you're unsure how to start a relationship. And you, Zeke, are disappointed because you don't know if you can have a decent relationship." (multiple responses of "Yeah, that's right.")

Mandy: "So what do we do?"

Lois: "Although your reasons are a little different, it seems that each of you is saying that you're frightened and hurt because you can't find a way to make new friends, and that each of you wants to start fresh, healthy relationships." (Lois looks at each person with an inquiring look. All nod their heads.)
"Or put another way, each of you is looking for a way to relate to other people without having to use drugs."

Mitch: "That's it exactly!" (multiple responses of "Yes!" and "That's it!")

Lois: "Although each of you might have slightly different reasons for developing friendships, we need to start with learning how to relate."

Frank: "We really have to start at the beginning."

Lois: "Exactly. Each of you has to learn to relate to another person as yourself rather than the way you are when you're high."

Zeke: "But how will we know if we're relating right or not?"

Lois: "You're looking for a way to tell if you're relating properly or not."

Mandy: "That's easy. For me, it's if the person wants to see me again."

Frank: "For me, it's if the person shares something special with me."

Zeke: "I guess for me it's if the person enjoys being with me."

Lois: "You haven't said anything, Mitch."

Mitch: "I don't know. I guess it's the same as with Mandy."

Lois: "Okay. Zeke, Frank, it seems that if someone is willing to see you again, more than likely that person enjoys your company and will be willing to be self-disclosing with you."

Zeke: "Yeah, I guess."

Frank: "Sure."

Lois: "So we can use the willingness of the other person to interact with you again as an indication of how well you're relating."

Mandy: "That'll be a real trick. I can't even get them to talk to me the first time!"

Lois: "It's hard for you to even get an initial conversation started. Well, the very first thing we need to learn is how to size people up to see if we want them as friends. Then we need to learn how to start the conversation to get them involved with us."

Mitch: "I never know what to say."

Lois: "Okay, so learning how to start a conversation makes sense for you. The next thing might be how to get them to talk about themselves."

Zeke: "Hey, yeah, if they think you're really interested in them they're more likely to become a friend."

Lois: "That's right. You're beginning to sound pleased with this. And the next step is getting them to want to intensify the relationship."

Mandy: "Can we really do this?"

Lois: "You're pretty surprised that learning how to make new friends is possible."

Mandy: "Hey, I thought I'd never be able to fit in with anyone but the freaks."

Lois: "You're feeling relieved because now there seems to be some hope."

Mandy: "When can we get started?"

Lois: "You want to get going right now?" (Zeke and Frank simultaneously, "Yeah!") "Okay. First we'll learn how to decide on who we want as new friends. Then we'll learn how to get them to talk about themselves. And finally we'll learn how to intensify a relationship."

Mitch: "You really can teach us that?"

Lois: "You're questioning if I can deliver what I've said. And yet you sound hopeful."

Mitch: "I really want to learn."

Lois: "And I want to teach you. We'll start right now. We'll probably need the next three sessions to teach you the skills."

Zeke: "I'm really excited. Maybe I can change my life."

Lois: "You're feeling relieved because you think you have a chance now."

When we initiate to impact our worlds in productive ways, we are growing. By the same powerful principle of reciprocity, we grow most in worlds that we have helped make growthful. In a *"chaining"* sequence, the helpers facilitate the helpees' growth; in turn, the helpees become helpers in relating to the world around them. This is the *"helper principle":* the ultimate test of helping is whether the helpee is transformed into a helper.

INITIATING ⟶ GROWING

4 Summary

Our only reason to live is to grow. "Human processing"—intrapersonal and interpersonal processing—is our vehicle to growth. We are the products of our "processing." Indeed, we are only human when we are "processing."

8.
RECYCLING THE HELPING PROCESS

This chapter addresses recycling the helping process to facilitate more extensive exploration, more accurate understanding, and more effective acting.

Read this case study. Based on your learnings about effective helping skills, review each helper response, and see if you can determine why each helper response is an effective one.

Case Study #5—Skilled Helping

HELPEE INVOLVING/ HELPER ATTENDING		TYPE OF RESPONSE
Floyd:	"Man, I don't see how this stuff is gonna get us anywhere! We've tried working together. We just can't get there from here."	
Helper:	"It's pretty frustrating to try working these things through without any one's help. If you're free the next hour, I'd like to get together with you in my office."	Informing
Tom:	"It's O.K. with me, I guess."	
Helper:	"What about you, Floyd? I'd like to spend a little time getting to know both of you better. Then I'll be able to be more helpful."	Encouraging
Floyd:	"What about a cup of coffee instead?"	

Helper:	"Coffee's fine. I can learn as much right here as in my office."	Attending Contextually
Floyd:	"What do you want to learn about us?"	
Tom:	"Yeah, I know you've been checkin' us out for quite a while."	
Helper:	"So you've been using your observation skills, too. You've noticed that I've really been paying attention to you."	Attending Personally
Tom:	"Uh huh. What have you been— you know—learning from us?"	
Helper:	"Well, I see two young guys who care enough about each other to stay in there fighting with each other. One's maybe more worn out than he should be and the other one's kind of edgy."	Observing
Floyd:	"You're really been using your eyes to see us, huh?"	
Helper:	(Pause) "And my ears to hear, too."	Listening

HELPEE EXPLORING/ HELPER RESPONDING

Floyd:	"The thing that really hassles me is the way you act like everything's cool and I'm just supposed to relax and keep smiling!"	
Helper:	"You're saying it really gets to you when white folks seem to want you to lay back and accept things."	Responding to Content

Tom:	"Man, we're all in this thing together! What's so special about you?"	
Helper:	"You don't see why Floyd has to make a special case out of himself."	Responding to Content
Floyd:	"You don't see it, huh Tom? Well maybe if you woke up black one morning a lot of things'd come clearer to you!"	
Helper:	"You feel angry."	Responding to Feeling
Floyd:	"Yeah, right! I mean, no white person can know what it's like to be black."	
Helper:	"You feel furious when someone who isn't black tries to tell you how to act."	Responding to Meaning
Tom:	"You got a lot of nerve to come on like that to me, man!"	
Helper:	"It makes you angry when Floyd doesn't seem to appreciate the way you act with him."	Responding to Meaning
Floyd:	"Listen, you get treated like an individual. But me—either I get turned down flat, or else everyone wants to get alongside of my blackness without ever checking out who I really am on the inside."	
Helper:	"It burns you up that people never seem to get past your skin to what's underneath."	Responding to Meaning
Floyd:	"Damn straight! I could be a genius or a flat-out fool and it still wouldn't matter as much as the fact that I'm black!"	

Helper: "It drives you wild because people just see how you look without ever caring what you do or how you feel."   *Responding to Meaning*

Tom: "Listen, you're doing the same thing when you lump me in with every other white!"

Helper: "You feel angry and frustrated because Floyd doesn't see the ways you try to relate to him as an individual."   *Responding to Meaning*

Floyd: "It's not the same thing, man. It's not like being black."

HELPEE UNDERSTANDING/ HELPER PERSONALIZING

Floyd: "They don't know who I am and they really aren't open to finding out."

Helper: "It really disrespects you because you're not seen as a real person.   *Personalizing Meaning*

Tom: "I'm trying—I really am, but for him I'm just another 'whitey.'"

Helper: "You're frustrated because you're just another white."   *Personalizing Meaning*

Floyd: "Listen! It's a burden—like having to run 10 miles just to warm up for a 100-yard dash. Like—well, take writing, for one. I tried to get on the board at the *Literary Magazine.* But once they found out I wasn't into writing heavy race-type stuff, they weren't interested."

Helper:	"It's infuriating because you can't find a way to get people to treat you like an individual in your own right."	Personalizing Problems
Tom:	"I feel the same way, man. If I could just convince you I really do see you as a person and not just a black."	
Helper:	"Tom, you feel disappointed because you can't get Floyd to see you as a real person—you're just another white guy to Floyd."	Personalizing Problems
Floyd:	"If I could just get through to people."	
Helper:	"You feel helpless because you can't get other people—especially Tom—to see you the way you really are."	Personalizing Feelings
Tom:	"In a way I'm in the same boat. Maybe I don't feel it as strongly as if I were black, but it seems like the same thing to me."	
Helper:	"You feel cheated because you can't get the real you across to Floyd."	Personalizing Feelings
Floyd:	"I've got a lot to offer. I mean really, I'm into a lot of good things I'd like to share. Like—well, like my writing."	
Helper:	"Floyd, you feel miserable because you can't get other people to see what you have to offer and you want to very badly."	Personalizing Goals

Tom: "Listen, Floyd, there's nothing I'd like more than for you and me to get beyond this lame race stuff. I'd like for you to trust me."

Helper: "And Tom, you feel pretty low because you can't get Floyd to understand you and you really want to get him to see beyond your whiteness."

Personalizing Goals

HELPEE ACTING/ HELPER INITIATING

Helper: "So Floyd, you want other people to see you as an individual. And Tom, you want Floyd to see you as an individual. How could you each tell if you were reaching those goals?"

Defining the Goals

Floyd: "A good indication for me would be if I could get on the board of the Literary Magazine without having to be the 'racial reporter.'"

Tom: "I'd just like to get rid of all my behaviors that Floyd feels are racist, so we can get beyond the color of our skins."

Helper: "O.K. Those sound like pretty realistic goals. Let's work on Floyd's program first. What might a first step be?"

Initiating First Step

Floyd: "Well, I could make out a list of things I'd like to do on the magazine."

Helper: "That's great! We call those values. If those are your values, what would the magazine's values be?" *Initiating Intermediate Steps*

Floyd: "That would be what the magazine would want a writer to do."

Helper: "Good! We call those requirements. So what do we do next?" *Initiating Intermediate Steps*

Floyd: "Well, obviously we've got to match up my values and their requirements—sort of like matching up columns A and B."

Helper: "So where they match, you . . ." *Initiating Final Steps*

Floyd: "I've got to show them what I can do for them—It's sort of like advertising yourself."

Helper: "That's nice and clean for you. Getting on the writing staff of the magazine is your goal. Your first step is values. Your intermediary steps are requirements and matching. Your final step is promoting or advertising yourself." *Summarizing Steps*

Floyd: "I can do that!"

Helper: You're confident in your program. It's sort of like testing yourself out." *Personalizing Meaning*

Floyd: "At least I'll find out if the problem is in them or in me."

Tom: "Or somewhere in between."

Helper: "That's where you think it might be with you and Floyd—somewhere in between you."

Tom: "Well, if I get the drift of your program, I might operate that same way: Personalizing Meaning

1. Set a goal of getting rid of racist attitudes and behaviors.
2. Do the first step of getting Floyd to make a list of my behaviors that he experiences as racist.
3. Do the intermediary steps of making a list of what I can handle and what I can't.
4. Get help from someone else for what I can't handle." Initiating Steps

Floyd: "You mean I won't have to hear the term "you people" anymore?"

Helper: "You really have it together now. That's a program that comes from the heart—out of your real motivation to change, Tom." Personalizing Meaning

Floyd: "I got to give you that, man!"

Helper: "You're both pretty excited about the possibilities." Personalizing Feelings

Tom: "And eager to get started!"

Floyd: "Maybe we won't have to have a revolution every generation."

Helper: "You're feeling hopeful because you're beginning to see how you can get there from here!" Personalizing Feelings

Recycling, as defined by *Webster's,* means to *bring back,* to *use again,* to *reuse.*

In recycling *intra*personal processing, we recycle the phases of learning; exploring where we are; understanding where we want or need to be; and acting to get from where we are to where we want or need to be. We recycle our *intra*personal processing to develop more effective responses. This is how we learn and grow.

With the feedback that we receive from the environment for our previous actions, we also recycle our interpersonal processing, our helping skills: responding to facilitate exploring more extensively; personalizing to facilitate understanding more accurately; and initiating to facilitate acting more effectively. We may use these helping skills with ourselves as well as with others. They will serve to facilitate our growth as well as the growth of those we help.

Phases of Interpersonal and *Intra*personal Processing

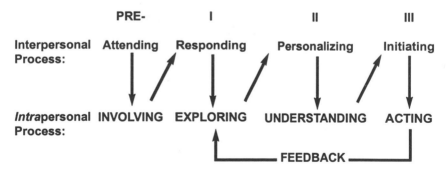

RECYCLING OUR INTERPERSONAL AND *INTRAPERSONAL* PROCESSES

Recycling Attending

To help others to recycle, or revisit, their involvement in the helping process, we recycle our attending skills. This means preparing the helpees, the context and ourselves for helping. This means attending personally by our physical posture and orientation. This means observing vigilantly and listening attentively. Although we have used these same skills before, we will find that in order to involve our helpees, we must revisit these simple yet profound skills.

We recycle skilled attending when we use feedback from our attending skills. We recycle skilled attending to stimulate or re-stimulate an increased level of helpee involvement in the helping process. Involvement by others is facilitated by recycling our attending skills.

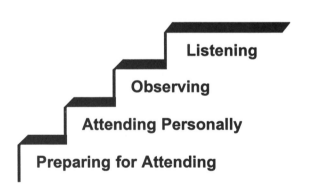

RECYCLING ATTENDING ➤ RECYCLING INVOLVEMENT

Recycling Responding

Helping others to recycle their exploration process involves formulating and communicating responses to the content, feeling and meaning of their experiences. Although we have used these same responding skills before, our responses are different each time we recycle the helping process. As helpers, we stay "in tune" with the new areas of exploration that our helpees want and need to explore.

When recycling skilled responding we are simply using feedback to stimulate more extensive exploring. We may facilitate the recycling of previously explored experiences or incorporate new presenting issues. Recycling exploration in others is facilitated by recycling our responding skills.

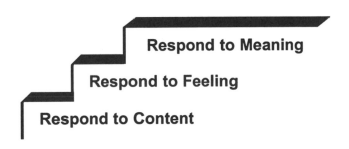

Respond to Meaning

Respond to Feeling

Respond to Content

RECYCLING RESPONDING ➡ RECYCLING EXPLORATION

Recycling Personalizing

Helping others to revisit their understanding process involves building upon an "interchangeable base" to formulate and communicate personalized responses to meaning, problems, goals and changing feelings. Although we have used these same personalizing skills before, our responses are different each time we recycle the helping process. As helpers, we must stay "in tune" with the new issues that our helpees want and need to understand.

When recycling skilled personalizing we are simply using feedback to stimulate more accurate understanding. We may facilitate the recycling of previously understood experiences or new understandings. Recycling understanding in others is facilitated by recycling or re-applying our personalizing skills.

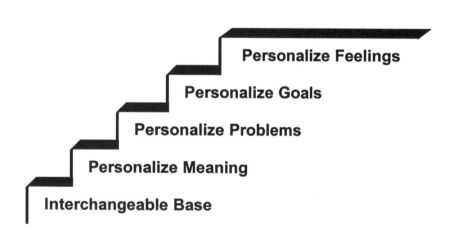

Personalize Feelings

Personalize Goals

Personalize Problems

Personalize Meaning

Interchangeable Base

RECYCLING PERSONALIZING ➞ RECYCLING UNDERSTANDING

Recycling Initiating

Helping others to recycle their action process involves defining, developing and initiating programs to achieve helpee goals. Although we have used these same initiating skills before, our responses are different each time we recycle the helping process. As helpers, we must stay "in tune" with the changing requirements that our helpees want and need to act upon.

When recycling skilled initiating we are simply using feedback to stimulate more effective acting. We may facilitate the recycling of previous actions goals, programs and steps, or new ones. Recycling acting by others is facilitated by recycling our initiating skills.

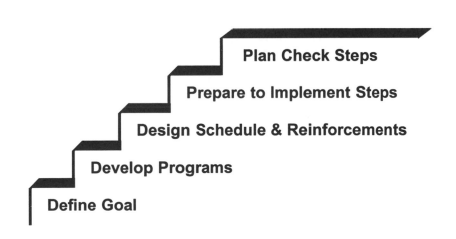

RECYCLING INITIATING → RECYCLING ACTING

Summary

We may want to conceptualize the helping process in terms that will remain with us: *attending, responding, personalizing* and *initiating* (A,R,P,I). If we know how each of these interpersonal helping skills relates to the phases of *intra*personal processing—*involvement, exploring, under-standing* and *acting* (I,E,U,A)—then we will never be lost in anything we do in life. Indeed, the critical incidents that are now crises for us become simply opportunities for recycling our skills.

LEVELS OF HELPING

5.0 Initiating
4.0 Personalizing
3.0 Responding
2.0 Attending
1.0 Nonattending

Now you know about the helping process. You will want to apply these skills throughout your life in all living, learning and working situations.

Case Study #6—Skilled Helping

Joan and Tom have been going steady for almost three years now. Joan is nineteen-years-old and is living at home with her parents. She has a part-time job in a retail store. Tom is also eighteen. He lives with his parents and works in a local restaurant. Tom has been working with a counselor at the community counseling center for the last month. We listen in as both Tom and Joan visit with a counselor.

HELPEE PROCESSING/ HELPER RECYCLING		TYPE OF RESPONSE
Tom:	"You know, I've tried to work things out with my parents. But things haven't worked out the way I rehearsed them."	
Helper:	"You're pretty upset because your rehearsals didn't pan out."	Responding to Meaning
Tom:	"Yeah. Maybe I didn't check myself out while I was attending to them, but I was really trying."	
Helper:	"You're also upset because some check steps got left out."	Responding to Meaning
Tom:	"Yeah. But I'm most disappointed in their reactions to me. I was really trying to attend to them like we practiced, but they kept holding me off."	
Helper:	"You're disappointed that they didn't receive your attentiveness."	Responding to Meaning

Tom:	"Maybe they're just not ready for it. Or suspicious of it."	
Helper:	"You're unsure because they may think you're only attentive to set them up for something bigger."	Responding to Meaning
Tom:	"It's true. I often did set them up in the past. Maybe they're just not ready for a change in me."	
Helper:	"You're really sad because you're left out of their lives."	Personalizing Meaning
Tom:	"Maybe it's me."	
Helper:	"You're really disappointed in yourself because you didn't bring it off with them."	Personalizing the Problem
Tom:	"My parents do mean a lot to me."	
Helper:	"You're committed to working things through with them."	Personalizing the Goal
Tom:	"Yeah. I'll revise my program and build in some more check steps. I'm gonna make it work."	
Helper:	"You're determined to follow through with them. Maybe we need to work on a step that lets them know that you're really trying to change—to help them become attentive with you."	Initiating a Step Program
Tom:	"I just wish my parents could get into listening instead of yelling at me all the time."	
Helper:	"You're saying that your parents holler a lot and don't pay much attention to what you have to say."	Responding to Content

Joan: "His parents and mine, too. Honestly, they treat us like we were little kids!"

Helper: "You feel pretty angry with them."

Responding to Feeling

Tom: "They're living in a dream world."

Helper: "It bugs you that they're so out of touch."

Responding to Meaning

Tom: "Yeah, and I just wish they'd let up on us."

Helper: "You really resent that they're always on your back."

Responding to Meaning

Joan: "We both do. See, we've been making some plans of our own. Only they won't believe that we're mature enough to handle things."

Helper: "It's frustrating when your parents don't accept your capabilities."

Responding to Meaning

Tom: "You know it! I mean, all we want to do is live together. That's no big thing today, right? But they act like such jerks, they think we're going to ruin our lives!"

Helper: "You feel furious because they won't let you make your own decisions."

Responding to Meaning

Joan: "Exactly! We've tried to show that we're responsible people, but it hasn't helped. I don't know how we're supposed to convince them that we can handle it."

Helper: "What it comes down to is that you are both fed up with the fact that they want you to live by their policies and you want to live your own lives on your own terms and not theirs."

Personalizing the Goal

Tom: "It's really a messed-up situation any way you look at it."

Helper: "It's a lousy feeling because even though you're pretty mad at your parents, you still care a lot about how they feel."

Personalizing Meaning

Joan: "Yeah, I've thought about that a lot."

Tom: "And now, because of all their negative comments, we're starting to wonder if they could be right. How can we help but wonder when our parents are making us look at the bad side all the time."

Helper: "So you're kind of uneasy, too, because you're not confident enough in yourself to be sure that moving in together would definitely be the right thing."

Personalizing Meaning

Joan: "For me it's like—well, when my parents tell me what to do, it makes me very defensive. But when I'm alone—I don't know— what if we went ahead and then found out we were making a mistake?"

Helper: "It concerns you because you can't figure out for sure what's the best thing for you both to do regardless of what others want you to do."

Personalizing the Problem

Tom: "Uh huh. I mean—well, I love Joan too much to want to do something for the wrong reason—just to get back at my parents, for example."

Helper: "It's scary because you can't be sure you're doing the right thing for the right reasons."

Personalizing the Feeling

Joan: "That's just it. I'm not sure we would even be so ready to live together if our parents weren't so set against it."

Helper: "You feel confused right now because you can't stop living in reaction to your parents even though you want to make decisions that reflect who you are."

Personalizing the Goal

Tom: "Yeah, we've got to be ourselves."

Helper: "You're certain you want to be yourselves even though you're sometimes not sure what that really means."

Personalizing Meaning

Helper: "It sounds to me like your goal isn't really to live together—but that you really want to find a way to make decisions based on your own values, rather than just reacting to others. What that means is being able to use your personal values to decide whether or not to live together."

Defining the Goal

Tom: "Yeah—but that's just it. Even when I know something is important, I can't seem to figure out what to do about it."

Helper: "It's irritating when you can't figure out how to live by your own values. The first thing you might do is explore your values and make a list of all the things that are important to you."

Initiating the First Step

Joan: "Sure—but how's that going to help us know what to do?"

Helper: "Well, once you know what's important, you can prioritize your values by deciding which one is most important, next important and so on—then you can use all this information to make the decision."

Initiating Intermediate Steps

Tom: "So you mean that some of our values ought to influence our decision more than others and that we have to know those values so we can make the best choice."

Helper: "That's right. When do you think you could make up a list of your values and priorities so we could get together and talk them over?"

Initiating Schedules

Joan: "We can get that done this afternoon and tonight."

Helper: "O.K. If you do that, then I'll meet
with you both again on Thursday
to review what you've done and
to show you how to use those
values systematically to make   Initiating
the best choices for you."   Reinforcements

Tom: "I think we're going to feel a
whole lot better once we've
worked this thing through."

Helper: "You already feel better just
knowing that you're going to be
able to make the best decision
based on the things that are   Personalizing
really important to you."   Meaning

Growth is life-long processing. A growing person is constantly involved in processing in an ongoing, ever expanding spiral of life. This spiral emphasizes our purposeful effort to constantly improve our functioning and our contributions to the world.

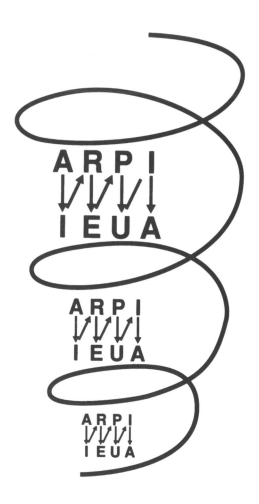

RECYCLING

The perspective with which we relate to this growth is human resource development. Not only does it facilitate helping, it also measures the effects of helping by performance. Likewise, helping is HRD's synergistic processing partner. Not only does helping facilitate HRD, it also provides the process for continuing HRD.

HRD ◄──► HELPING

HRD ◄──► HELPING

EPILOGUE

To the Reader upon Closing This Book:

Together, we have reviewed the past and brought ourselves up to the present. I hope in the process that we have learned the core interpersonal skills of helping. What about the future? How can you prepare for it? Where might you fit in it?

Think about it for a minute! For almost all of humankind's 14-million-year history, people have relied almost exclusively upon reflexive conditioned responding. Only the occasional thinker has fashioned "breakthroughs" in science and technology and art which have changed the course of civilization. With the environment evolving ever so slowly, the response to most changes was to apply the conditioned responses with greater intensity and quantity—to "Work Harder!" Neither the farming technologies of the Agrarian Age nor the mechanical technologies of the Industrial Age altered the emphasis upon conditioned responding.

It was not until about thirty years ago that the Electronics Era and then the Data Age introduced new requirements for human processing. Instead of non-thinking linear conditioning, the complexities of design and technology required multidimensional, discriminative learning: the ability to discriminate multiple dimensions of stimulus inputs, select the appropriate responses, and emit these responses behaviorally. This meant that human processors needed to become a repository of "branching" responses from which they would draw to discriminate stimuli and emit responses. With the environment changing increasingly rapidly, people needed to develop response-sharing strategies that would increase the response repertories of the human processors. This is when interpersonal communication skills came into the picture: they facilitated the consensus and response-building strategies that dominate us today. We labeled our ability to mount responses to known stimuli, "Working Smarter," and it worked—for a while!

The problem is that, due to accelerating innovation, the environment is changing more rapidly than we can develop and disseminate responses. Indeed, changes are spiraling and time is telescoped! The only course available to us is to develop and empower people in generative processing skills: skills that enable the processor to generate totally new responses to stimuli, responses that the stimuli were not calculated to elicit. Generative processing brings with it a whole new set of requirements for human processors: the humans have to become a repository of thinking skills—individual, interpersonal and interdependent thinking skills. We call our ability to generate entirely new responses, "Thinking Better," and it will yield whole new Ages of Information and Ideation.

These are the changes and the requirements being imposed upon us—right now! How do you prepare yourself for this? How do you fit in?

Well, think of the interpersonal paradigm that you have just learned: attending, responding, personalizing, initiating. Now think of the intra*personal processing that these interpersonal skills facilitate: involving, exploring, understanding, acting. These phases of processing yield the basic ingredients of generative processing. When we put the power of generative processing inside of people, then we enable them to generate entirely new responses. To be sure, when we empower people with generative processing skills, we empower them to generate entirely new stimulus environments.*

What only random thinkers did throughout the history of humankind, we will all do. What only an occasional relator did, we will all do. What very rare interdependent processors did, we will all do. We will all become generative processors.

That is the future—if there is to be a future for us at all!

That is how you prepare for it—if you entertain becoming whole!

That is how you fit in it—if you can contemplate generating your own destiny and helping others to generate theirs.

Growthfully yours,

Bob Carkhuff

Appendices

APPENDIX A: FEELING WORD LIST

Happy	Sad	Angry	Confused
alive	awful	agitated	anxious
amused	bad	annoyed	awkward
anxious	blue	bitter	baffled
calm	bummed out	burned up	bewildered
cheerful	crushed	critical	bothered
content	depressed	disgusted	crazy
delighted	desperate	dismayed	dazed
ecstatic	devastated	enraged	disorganized
elated	disappointed	envious	disoriented
energized	dissatisfied	fed up	distracted
excited	distressed	frustrated	disturbed
fantastic	disturbed	furious	embarrassed
fortunate	down	hostile	frustrated
friendly	embarrassed	impatient	helpless
fulfilled	gloomy	irate	hopeless
glad	glum	irritated	jolted
good	hateful	livid	lost
great	hopeless	mad	mixed up
hopeful	hurt	outraged	panicky
lively	lonely	perturbed	paralyzed
loving	lost	put out	perplexed
motherly	low	riled	puzzled
optimistic	miserable	resentful	shocked
overjoyed	painful	seething	stuck
peaceful	sorry	sore	stunned
pleased	terrible	ticked off	surprised
proud	turned off	uptight	tangled
refreshed	uneasy	worked up	trapped
relaxed	unhappy		troubled
relieved	unloved		uncertain
rested	upset		uncomfortable
satisfied			undecided
spirited			unsure
thankful			upset
thrilled			weak
turned on			
up			
warm			
wonderful			

Scared

afraid
anxious
apprehensive
awed
cautious
chicken
edgy
fearful
frightened
hesitant
horrified
insecure
intimidated
jumpy
lonely
nervous
panicky(ed)
shaky
tense
terrified
threatened
timid
uneasy
unsure
worried

Weak

ashamed
blocked
bored
defenseless
demoralized
disorganized
distracted
discouraged
embarrassed
exhausted
fragile
frail
frustrated
guilty
helpless
horrible
ill
impotent
inadequate
incapable
insecure
lifeless
lost
overwhelmed
powerless
quiet
run-down
shaky
shy
sick
small
stressed
stupid
timid
tired
unsure
useless
vulnerable
worn out

Strong

active
aggressive
alert
angry
bold
brave
capable
confident
determined
eager
energetic
happy
healthy
intense
loving
mean
open
positive
potent
powerful
quick
secure
solid
spirited
super
sure
tough

APPENDIX B: HCD LEVELS OF FUNCTIONING

The HRD profile emphasizing levels of functioning within areas and dimensions of HRD resource components appears in Table 2. The nature, evolution and applications of these dimensions are developed fully in *HCD XXI—Human Capital Development in the 21st Century.*

TABLE 2
HCD PROFILE

AREAS AND DIMENSIONS

LEVELS OF FUNCTIONING	PHYSICAL	EMOTIONAL			INTELLECTUAL		
	PHYSICAL FITNESS	PERSONAL MOTIVATION	INTERPERSONAL RELATING	INFORMATIONAL RELATING	INFORMATIONAL REPRESENTING	INTELLECTUAL PROCESSING
5 LEADER	STAMINA	MISSION	INITIATING	STANDARD	MULTI-D	ACTING
4 CONTRIBUTOR	INTENSITY	ACTUALIZATION	PERSONALIZING	CONDITIONS	NESTED-D	UNDERSTANDING
3 PARTICIPANT	ADAPTABILITY	ACHIEVEMENT	RESPONDING	PROCESSES	3D	EXPLORING
2 OBSERVER	SURVIVABILITY	INCENTIVE	ATTENDING	COMPONENTS	2D	GOALING
1 DETRACTOR	SICKNESS	NON-INCENTIVE	NON-ATTENDING	FUNCTIONS	1D	NON-PREPARATION

APPENDIX C: THE CARKHUFF HELPING MODEL
Research Background

Helping Outcomes

Historically, Eysenck (1960) and others (Levitt, 1963; Lewis, 1965) confronted the helping professions with the challenge that counseling and psychotherapy really did not make a difference. About two-thirds of the patients remained out of the hospital a year after treatment, whether or not they were seen by professional psychotherapists. These effects held for adult and child treatment.

One answer to this challenge was the finding that the variability, or range of effects, of the professionally treated groups on a variety of psychological indices was significantly greater than the variability of the "untreated" groups (Rogers, Gendlen, Kiesler, & Truax, 1967; Truax & Carkhuff, 1967). This meant that professional practitioners tended to spread their effects on the patients. This suggested one very consoling conclusion: Counseling and psychotherapy really did make a difference. It also suggested one very distressing conclusion: Counseling and psychotherapy have a two-edged effect—they may be helpful or harmful (Bergin, 1971).

Follow-up research by Anthony and his associates (Anthony, Buell, Sharratt, & Althoff, 1972; Anthony, Cohen, & Vitalo, 1978) shed some light on the lasting effects of counseling, rehabilitation and psychotherapeutic techniques. This research was based upon data indicating that within three to five years of treatment 65 percent to 75 percent of the ex-psychiatric patients would once again be patients. Also, regardless of the follow-up period, the gainful employment of ex-patients would be below 25 percent.

The major conclusion drawn from these data on outcome was that counseling and psychotherapy—as traditionally practiced—was effective in about 20 percent of the cases. Of the two-thirds of the clients and patients who initially got better, only one-third to one-quarter stayed better. Multiplied out, this meant that psychotherapy had lasting positive effects in between 17 percent and 22 percent of the cases. Counseling and psychotherapy may indeed be "for better or for worse." In most instances, the lasting effects are not facilitative.

In order to understand the reasons for these outcomes, we examined the process of counseling and psychotherapy. When we looked at effective helping processes from the perspective of the helpee, we found that helping is simply a learning or relearning process leading to change or gain in the behavior of the helpee (Bergin, 1971; Carkhuff, 1969).

Learning Processes

The phases of effective counseling and psychotherapy are really the phases of effective learning (Carkhuff, 1969, 1971a; Carkhuff & Berenson, 1967, 1977). The helping processes by which helpees are facilitated or retarded in their development involve their exploring where they are in their worlds; understanding and specifying where they want to be; and developing and implementing step-by-step action programs to get there.

Exploring is a pre-condition of understanding, giving both helper and helpee an opportunity to get to know the helpee's experience of where he or she is in the world. In this respect, exploration is a self-diagnostic process for the helpee. Exploration is in part under the control of the helper and in part under the control of the helpee. High-level functioning helpees explore themselves independent of the level of interpersonal skills offered by the helpers while moderate to low-level functioning helpees are dependent upon the helper's skills for their level of exploration (Carkhuff & Berenson, 1976).

Understanding is the necessary mediational process between exploring and acting (Carkhuff & Berenson, 1976). It serves to help the client focus upon personalized goals made available through exploration. The basic foundation for understanding rests with insights—insights revealing the helpee's own deficits and role in the situation—which increase the probability that related behaviors will occur. Unfortunately, action does not always follow insight. For one thing, insights promoted by "common sense" techniques are usually neither developed systematically (in such a way that each piece of explored material is used as a base for the next level of understanding) nor with specificity as observable, measurable, repeatable behavior; therefore, the individual helpee, aided only by common sense, does not "own" the insights and cannot act upon them.

Acting is the necessary culminating process of helping (Carkhuff & Berenson, 1976). The helpees must act upon their newly personalized understanding in order to demonstrate a change or gain in their behavior. In doing so, they are provided with the opportunity to acquire new experience and thus stimulate more extensive exploration, more accurate understanding, and more effective action. Any discrepancy between understanding and acting is, in part, a function of the lack of systematically developed action programs that flow from systematically developed insights.

In conclusion, both helpers and helping programs are effective in facilitating the helping process to the degree that they incorporate and emphasize the phases of learning: involving the helpees in exploring where they are in their worlds; understanding and specifying goals for where they want or need to be; and developing and implementing step-by-step action programs to achieve their goals. The helpers who have the helping skills and the skills to develop helping programs are, for the most part, those individuals who have learned them in systematic skills-training programs, whether professional or paraprofessional (Anthony & Carkhuff, 1978; Carkhuff, 1968).

The number of models of helping based upon this simple paradigm of helping as learning have proliferated in the literature of counseling and psychotherapy (Anthony, 1979; Brammer, 1973; Combs, Avila, & Purkey, 1978; Danish & Hauer, 1973; Egan, 1975, 1990; Gazda, 1973; Goodman, 1972; Guerney, 1977; Ivey & Authier, 1978; Kagan, 1975; Patterson, 1973; Schulman, 1974). Through varying their terminology, most attribute the effectiveness of counseling and psychotherapy to those helper skills that facilitate the helpee's self-exploration. None of these helping approaches has identified and operationalized the helper dimensions of personalizing that culminate in helpee action and behavior change. Indeed, most major therapeutic orientations tend to emphasize exclusively one phase of helping or the other.

And what about the "common sense" approach to helping that is employed by the well-intentioned, yet unskilled helper? Perhaps the best illustration of the potential dangers and harm of the "common sense" approach are several research studies that investigated the helping skills of untrained hot-line volunteers (Carothers & Inslee, 1974; Augelli, Handis, Brumbaugh, Illig, Shearer, Turner & Frankel, 1978; Genther, 1974; Rosenbaum & Calhoun, 1977; Schultz, 1975). Volunteers such as these would certainly seem to be concerned and well-intended. Yet despite such assumptions, the research suggests that untrained volunteers do not normally possess a high level of helping skills to combine with their good intentions. In order to be effective, helpers must combine their good intentions with helping skills; for it is the helper's skills that make the difference. Concern is clearly not enough. None of this is intended to imply that volunteers or other types of noncredentialed helpers cannot be expert in the skills of helping. As a matter of fact, uncredentialed helpers who have buttressed their good intentions with a training program in helping skills can be as helpful or more helpful than the typical credentialed professional (Anthony & Carkhuff, 1978; Carkhuff, 1968).

Attending Skills

At the pre-helping or involvement stage of helping, the helping skills are essentially nonverbal. Except for the preliminary attending skills of informing and encouraging, these are all skills that the helper does "without opening his or her mouth." Perhaps because of the lack of verbal involvement, these attending skills are sometimes considered to be relatively simple and unimportant. Yet a number of research investigations suggest that these skills are more potent and more complex than is generally believed (Barker, 1971; Birdwhistell, 1967; Carkhuff, 1969; Ekman, Friesen, & Ellsworth, 1972; Hall, 1959, 1976; Ivey & Authier, 1978; Mehrabian, 1972; Schefflen, 1969; Truax & Carkhuff, 1967).

Getting and Keeping the Helpee Involved

It would seem that helpee involvement in the helping process should be a foregone conclusion. After all, helping is for the helpee—why not become involved? Unfortunately, significant data exist that indicate the helpee involvement is far from the norm (McClurek, 1978), suggesting, perhaps, that the helpee may not perceive helping as being totally for his or her own benefit.

For example, one study reported data that indicated that as many as 66 percent of the patients referred from a psychiatric hospital to a community-based rehabilitation center chose not to attend the center (Wolkon, 1970). In addition, only half of those persons who began the program attended more than ten times. Other researchers have summarized data that indicated that a large number of clients prematurely drop out of counseling and psychotherapy of their own volition (Garfield, 1971). One such study found that of the 13,450 clients seen in nineteen community mental health facilities, approximately 40 percent terminated treatment after only one session, and that the dropout rate for the nonwhite clients was significantly higher (Sue, McKinney, & Allen, 1976; Sue, McKinney, Allen, & Hall, 1974). Clearly, helpee involvement in the helping process cannot be taken for granted.

Positioning, Observing and Listening

Some researchers (Genther & Moughan, 1977; Smith-Hanen, 1977) have investigated how different aspects of the helper's positioning skills affect how the helper is evaluated by the helpee. For example, Smith-Hanen (1977) found that certain leg and arm positions of the counselor do affect the helpee's judgment of counselor warmth and empathy. Genther and Moughan (1977) examined the effect of the counselor's forward leaning (incline) on the helpee's rating of attentiveness. In all instances, the helper in the forward-leaning position was evaluated by the helpees as more attentive than the helper in an upright posture.

Additional research suggests that, besides attempting to get and keep the helpee involved, the positioning skills of the helper are also important because of their critical relationship to observing skills (Carkhuff, 1969). This relationship between helper positioning and observing skills is apparent in several key ways. First, an attentive posture and an appropriate environment facilitate observing, primarily by reducing the observer's possible distractions. Second, by making observations of a helpee's attending position, a helper can draw possible inferences about the helpee's feeling state and energy level. Third, positioning oneself so that you can pay attention to people can make people more nonverbally expressive, eliciting more nonverbal material to observe and more verbal material to which to listen and from which to make inferences.

Research findings in the area of verbal and nonverbal communication support the contention that there is a relationship between positioning, observing and listening skills (Barker, 1971; Mehrabian, 1972). Just as the helper's observing skills are in part a function of her or his positioning skills, a helper's listening skills are related to the skillfulness with which he or she positions himself or herself and observes. As a matter of fact, observing can be conceived of as a type of nonverbal listening. A person who demonstrates that she or he is listening nonverbally (observing) will increase the verbal output of the speaker. Additional research findings suggest that it is the listener's combined use of both observing and listening skills that allows the listener to identify discrepancies and incongruities between the speaker's verbal and nonverbal behaviors. The discovery of this type of discrepancy is an issue that the helper and helpee will ultimately have to deal with in the later phases of counseling.

In terms of listening skills, common sense would tell us that, because we have spent so much of our time in listening situations, we should be very good at it. (Approximately 40 percent of a person's daily verbal interaction is spent in listening.) Unfortunately, communication research suggests that immediately after listening to a short talk, a person remembers only one-half of what he or she has heard. This is not because the listener has not had time to listen. Most people are capable of comprehending speech at a rate three to four times faster than normal conversation. Thus the listener has plenty of time to think. The key to effective listening appears to be how the listener uses her or his extra "thinking time."

In summary, the research evidence suggests that the pre-helping skills of positioning, observing and listening appear to be both cumulative and causative skills. First of all, these pre-helping skills are cumulative in that the helper can improve his or her observing skills through careful positioning; similarly, a helper can improve her or his listening skills by observing and positioning well. Second, these pre-helping skills are causative in terms of their effect on the helpee.

Preparing increases the chances of the helpee appearing for help. The helpee who appears for help becomes the subject of the helper's constant positioning skills, which in turn facilitates the helpee's expression of nonverbal behavior. The helpee, as he or she expresses himself or herself nonverbally, becomes the subject of the helper's observing skills, which in turn facilitate the helpee's verbal expressions. The verbal expressions of the helpee become the target of the helper's listening skills. Finally, it is this combination of the helper's preparing, positioning, observing and listening skills that facilitates the helpee's expression of personally relevant material to which the helper must skillfully respond.

Responding Skills

Most major theoretical orientations to counseling and psychotherapy have recognized the importance of the patient talking about what is troubling him or her. In particular, Freud (1924) popularized a "talking cure" for emotional problems, while Rogers, Gendlin, Kiesler, & Truax (1967) strongly stressed the necessity of helpee self-exploration. In addition to these theoretical emphases, a great deal of research has been amassed that indicates a significant positive relationship between the degree of helpee self-exploration and therapeutic outcome. That is, those helpees who talk in greater detail about their unique problems and situations are more apt to improve over the course of helping.

One of the reasons for the increasing number of studies on helpee self-exploration has been the development of reliable and observable rating scales by means of which the dimension of self-exploration can be analyzed. The most widely used scale of self-exploration, upon which countless numbers of research investigations have been carried out, can be found in Robert R. Carkhuff's *Helping and Human Relations, Volume 2* (1969 & 1984).

Effects of Helper Responding Skills on Helpee Exploration

Perhaps one of the most significant scientific discoveries in therapeutic research is that certain skills the helper uses directly influence the degree to which a helpee will explore personally relevant material (Carkhuff, 1969; Rogers et al., 1967; Truax & Carkhuff, 1967). These helper skills, once referred to as the facilitative conditions of empathy, respect, and genuineness, are now operationalized in the helper skill of responding. A series of experimental studies found that a helper can deliberately increase and decrease the helpee's depth of self-exploration by directly changing the level of the helper's responding skills (Cannon & Pierce, 1968; Holder, Carkhuff, & Berenson, 1967; Piaget et al., 1967; Truax & Carkhuff, 1965). The research results show that when the helpers were most responsive, the helpees' self-exploration was much more personally relevant; when these same helpers became less responsive, the helpees' exploration became less personal. In addition, the effects of relatively unskilled helpers on helpee self-exploration were also studied. Investigators discovered that the helper who is unskilled in responding will, over time, decrease her or his helpees' level of self-exploration.

This is not to say that the helpee does not have a role to play in how willing he or she is to explore personally relevant material. Some helpees are certainly more willing to explore themselves than are other helpees. However, the research supports the belief that, irrespective of the helpees' own ability and willingness to explore, the responding skills of the helper can directly influence helpee self-exploration; and helpees who have helpers who are unskilled in responding will gradually introduce less and less personally relevant material into the helping interaction.

Although a helper can certainly do more than just use her or his responding skills, responsive skills in and of themselves, can, at times, have a differential effect on helpee outcome.

Several experimental studies have demonstrated that the outcome of a conditioning or a reinforcement program was found to be, in part, a function of the level of responding skills exhibited by the experimenter/helper (Mickelson & Stevic, 1971; Murphy & Rowe, 1977; Vitalo, 1970).

Undoubtedly the most significant and meaningful finding with respect to the relationship between responding skills and helping outcome has been made in the field of education. Over the past two decades, one finding has consistently emerged from educational research: a positive relationship exists between the teacher's responding skills and various measures of student achievement and other educational outcomes (Aspy, 1973; Aspy & Roebuck, 1977; Carkhuff, 1971 a; Carkhuff & Berenson, 1976; Truax & Carkhuff, 1967). Thus a teacher's ability to respond to her or his students will affect how much those students learn. More recent studies have shown that a teacher's responding skills are not only positively related to education outcome criteria but also to criteria that have primarily been the goals of guidance counselors and other mental health professionals—criteria like improved student self-concept and decreased student absenteeism.

In summary, the skilled helper, regardless of his or her theoretical orientation, has much to gain by using responding skills. First, the use of responding skills will directly influence the amount of personally relevant material the helpee will express to the helper. Second, helpers who are trying to get their helpees to learn certain skills or follow a certain program will improve the outcomes of their helping programs if they are able to respond skillfully to the helpees' experiences.

Personalizing Skills

Research has shown that there are skills beyond responding that a helper can use to assist the helpee to develop personal insights into his or her unique situation (Carkhuff, 1969,1971 a; Carkhuff & Berenson, 1977; Truax & Carkhuff, 1967). In other words, the skills of responding are usually necessary but rarely sufficient. It is typically not enough for the helper to see the world only through the helpee's eyes. The helpee is often unable to develop the necessary insights by herself or himself; at these times, the helper must use interpretive skills to go beyond what the helpee can do on his or her own.

What is needed is a transitional stage between helpee exploration and helpee action. This stage is understanding. It is a stage in which the helpee comes to "personalize" or "individualize" his or her problems and goals. The helper's task during the understanding phase is to formulate and communicate the helpee's personalized problems and goals (Carkhuff & Berenson, 1977). This personalized understanding relates the helpee's exploration to action programs that the helpee wants and needs. Personalizing helps the helpee to programmatically develop insights into his or her problems and goals before embarking upon an action course.

A rather ingenious study examined the relationship between a therapist's theoretical orientation and the level of personalizing skills that he or she demonstrates in a counseling interview. The study divided the professional therapists (all M.D.'s and Ph.D.'s) into three major theoretical orientations—psychodynamic, behavioristic, and humanistic—based on the therapists' own stated preferences. Each therapist tape recorded an actual interview with a pseudo-client. Ratings of the therapists' personalizing skills evidenced no significant differences between therapists of any of the three theoretical orientations, even though theoretically one would expect their levels of personalizing skills to differ (Fischer, Pavenza, Kickertz, Hubbard, & Grayston, 1975).

These research studies, as well as the current plethora of counseling theories, have a fairly straightforward implication for the development of counselor personalizing skills. That is, it would certainly be premature to make interpretations based exclusively on any one theory of psychotherapy. It would appear that at the present state of our research and theoretical knowledge, it would be most effective to assume an eclectic theoretical stance. The "appropriateness" of any theory is a function of how well the theoretical perspective allows the helper to make personalized responses to the helpee—a personalized response to which the helpee can understand and agree—which in turn sets the stage for effective helpee action, which is the next phase of the helping process.

One series of studies was undertaken to assess whether counselors who were able to demonstrate their responsive and interpretive skills with a client were different in any other ways from helpers whose best responses demonstrated only attending, listening and/or responding skills (Anthony, 1971). To ensure that counselors in the study would be functioning at interpersonal skill levels greater than the average counselor, this study used counselors who had just received a 30-hour interpersonal skills training experience. Each counselor conducted a 30 to 40 minute interview with the same physically disabled client. Comparisons between counselors who were rated as functioning at relatively higher levels of interpersonal skills versus those counselors who were functioning at slightly lower levels indicated that the higher level counselors outperformed their relatively lower level functioning counterparts on four indices: (1) client's depth of self-exploration; (2) counselor's level of immediacy after confrontations by the client; (3) counselor's use of confrontation; and (4) counselor's score on a test reflecting the favorability of the counselor's attitude toward physically disabled persons. The results of this study suggest that meaningful differences exist between those counselors who possess both responding and interpretive or personalizing skills and those who do not. Particularly significant is the fact that the high-functioning group of counselors had a greater effect on a client-process measure related to counseling outcome (client self-exploration).

Another series of experimental studies investigated one such instance when it is necessary for the helper to become additive in his or her understanding, that is, when the helpee becomes reluctant to engage in any further self-exploration (Alexik & Carkhuff, 1967; Carkhuff & Alexik, 1967). In these research studies the client, unknown to the therapists involved, was given a mental set to explore herself deeply during the first third of an interview, to talk only about irrelevant and impersonal details during the middle third, and to explore herself deeply again during the final third of the interview. The research data indicated that in the middle third of the session, when the client began to "run away" from the therapeutic encounter, the most responsive therapists began to become more interpretive, more immediate, and more confronting; overall, more personalized in their understanding of the helpee's immediate problems.

The skill of confrontation is a therapeutic technique that can be one of the most potent (albeit one of the most abused) interpretive skills. Berenson and Mitchell (1974) have comprehensively researched and analyzed the unique contributions of the skill of confrontation. Their ground-breaking efforts in this area have led to many specific conclusions including the following: (a) that helpers who have a higher level of responsive skills confront in a different and more effective manner than helpers who possess low levels of responsive skills; (b) that there are different types of confrontation that can be used most effectively when applied in a certain sequence; and (c) that confrontation, in and of itself, is never a sufficient therapeutic skill.

A number of approaches to counseling and psychotherapy emphasize the understanding phase of helping. Best known, of course, are the psychoanalytic and neo-analytic positions (Adler, 1927; Brill, 1938; Freud, 1924, 1933; Fromm, 1947; Homey, 1945; Jones, 1953; Jung, 1939; Mullahy, 1948; Rank, 1929; Sullivan, 1948).

Most modern psychoanalysts and psychiatrists, whose predominant technique is psychoanalysis, recognize that although psychoanalytic theory may have contributed to the beginnings of an understanding of human thoughts and feelings, many of the techniques and assumptions of classical analysis are no longer adequate (Loran, 1972; Freund, 1972; Conn, 1973; Friedman, 1975; McLaughlin, 1978; Older, 1977). With their basic assumption concerning the evil nature of mankind, the classical psychoanalytic position emphasized analyzing away client destructiveness. The final irony is that "after peeling back the trappings and exposing the undergarments of an ugly world, Freud found no alternatives" (Carkhuff & Berenson, 1967, p. 107). The psychoanalytic positions had no real constructive alternatives to offer.

Some of the existential approaches to therapy attempted to fill this void by offering their cosmologies as alternatives to the psychoanalysts' assumptions of pathology (Binswanger, 1956; Boss, 1963; Heidegger, 1962; May, 1961). Unfortunately, in the process of maximizing the emphasis upon honest encounter in the exchange of cosmologies, the existential approaches minimized the role definition of the helper. Thus, paradoxically, they failed to define the skills that are part and parcel of any effective cosmology (Carkhuff & Berenson, 1977).

There are a number of helping orientations that offer constructs or "handles" that may be useful in expanding the helpees' insights into what they are doing to contribute to their problems. The effective helper may draw from a variety of systems when helping to personalize the understanding of the helpee. The limit of simply exchanging one cosmology for another, however, is that the helpers are asking the helpees to fit their models of functioning rather than to develop the models to fit the helpees. A helper must be open to new orientations yet always oriented to observable and measurable effectiveness for each individual helpee. Personalizing skills offer helpers an opportunity to work with helpees to overcome personalized problems and achieve personalized goals in their lives.

Initiating Skills

One of the reasons why the continual challenges to the efficacy of counseling and psychotherapy have not been completely answered is that therapists have typically not defined their goals in observable terms. For example, helpers often describe helpees as needing to become more motivated, adjusted, self-actualized, self-accepting, congruent, insightful and so on. These goals certainly do not describe an observable activity; as a result, their achievement would be difficult to document and verify. The critics of psychotherapy have not claimed that psychotherapy is ineffective; rather, they have pointed out that the evidence that does exist has failed to indicate that psychotherapy IS EFFECTIVE (Eysenck, 1972). In other words, the burden of proof is on the provider of the service; and unless therapeutic goals are defined as meaningful, observable and measurable, then therapeutic effectiveness is difficult to document.

Defining Goals Can Get Results

The ability to define or operationalize goals, then, is the key to the effective action-steps that the helpee must take (Carkhuff, 1969, 1984). A goal is defined in terms of the operations required to achieve it. A goal is, therefore, observable, measurable and achievable (Carkhuff, 1974, 1985 a).

Perhaps one of the most intriguing findings with respect to the skill of goal definition is that simply requiring the therapist to set observable goals seems to improve therapeutic outcome in and of itself. In an experimental study of the benefits of goal definition, Smith (1976) had one group of adolescent helpees counseled by professional therapists in their own style with one notable exception: the therapists had been instructed in how to define observable goals for their helpees. Another group of therapists counseled their helpees without receiving prior training in defining observable helpee goals. At the end of eight counseling sessions, the group of helpees aided by counselors who had defined observable goals showed significantly greater improvement on a variety of counseling outcome indices. In an entirely different study, client satisfaction and subsequent prediction of recidivism was found to be related to client goal-attainment (Wilier & Miller, 1978).

Walker (1972), in studying an agency designed to rehabilitate the hardcore unemployed, found that, when feedback to the helpers about how well their helpees were achieving observable rehabilitation goals was experimentally withdrawn, the number of helpees rehabilitated decreased; likewise, when the helpers were once again provided feedback as to how well their helpees were achieving their goals, the helping outcome improved once again. In other words, the setting of observable helpee goals combined with feedback to the helpers in terms of how well the helpees are achieving these goals can, in and of itself, improve an agency's helping outcome. Other researchers have reported similar positive effects of goal-setting training in improving general job performance (Latham & Rinne, 1974; Bucker, 1978; Erez, 1977; Holroyd & Goldenberg, 1978; Flowers & Goldman, 1976).

In summary, flowing from the helpee's extensive exploration of where he or she is, the helping process converges in the helpee's understanding of the goals for where he or she wants or needs to be. The ability to achieve these goals is a function of the ability to define or operationalize each goal. Given the time and the resources, any goal that can be operationally defined can be achieved.

Teaching as Treatment

In 1971, Carkhuff suggested that training clients directly in the skills that they need to function in society would be a potent treatment method. In other words, once the helper established an effective therapeutic relationship, identified with the helpee what specific goals needed to be attained, and developed the necessary program steps, the helper would then involve the helpee in skills-training programs designed to achieve these goals. As a helper moves from training individual clients to teaching groups of clients, the helper-teacher must be much more knowledgeable about those teaching skills needed by the helper to facilitate the skill-learning process of groups of clients (Carkhuff & Berenson, 1976).

Interestingly enough, some of the most ingenious skills-training programs have been developed to systematicallly teach clients the same relationship skills that the effective helper uses in the helping process. That is, skills-training programs have been developed to teach clients how to respond to others and themselves in a skillful manner so that these clients may function more effectively in interpersonal situations.

Some of the earliest skills-training programs trained psychiatric inpatients in responding skills (Pierce & Drasgow, 1969; Vitalo, 1971). Both of these studies found that psychiatric patients could be trained to function at higher levels of interpersonal skills and that these trained patients achieved a higher level of interpersonal functioning than a variety of control and other treatment conditions. Similar results have been found in training parents (Carkhuff & Bierman, 1970; Reed, Roberts, & Forehand, 1977) and mixed racial groups (Carkhuff & Banks, 1970).

No doubt one of the most comprehensive studies of the effects of a training-as-treatment approach has been the changeover of an entire institution for delinquent boys from a custodial to a skills-training orientation (Carkhuff, 1974). Correctional personnel with no credentials in mental health were trained in interpersonal, problem-solving and program-development skills. Using the skills, the correctional personnel helped develop and deliver more than eighty skills-training programs in a variety of physical, emotional and intellectual areas of functioning.

The results achieved by these correctional personnel were quite dramatic, indicating that they were able to bring about a kind of inmate change of which credentialed mental health professionals would be justifiably proud. A summary of the various outcome criteria used indicates that the delinquents' physical functioning increased 50 percent, their emotional functioning 100 percent, and their intellectual functioning 15 percent. The physical functioning measure assessed seven categories of physical fitness as developed by the American Association for Health, Physical Education and Recreation; the emotional functioning measure involved a rating of the juveniles' human relations skills; intellectual functioning was measured by the California Achievement Test. In addition to the gains in physical, emotional and intellectual functioning, during a one-year period, "Elopement" status decreased 56 percent, recidivism rates decreased 34 percent, and crime in the community surrounding the institution decreased 34 percent.

Following this study an extensive number of programs utilizing teaching as a preferred mode of treatment with problem youth were reported. For example, delinquent youth with low levels of living, learning and working skills were trained in those skills. The results yielded recidivism rates of approximately 10 percent after one year and 20 percent after two years, against base rates for the control groups of 50 percent and 70 percent, respectively (Collingwood, Douds, Williams, & Wilson, 1978).

In addition, youthful minority-group dropout learners were taught "how-to-learn reading and mathematics skills." The results indicated that the students were able to gain one year or more in intellectual achievement in twenty-six two-hour sessions (Berenson, Berenson, Berenson, Carkhuff, Griffin, & Ransom, 1978). Clearly, teaching is a preferred mode of treatment in both preventative and rehabilitative modalities.

The Carkhuff Helping Model

The research of helping skills demonstrations over two decades is summarized in Table 1 (Carkhuff, 1983). As can be seen in Table 1, 164 studies were reported with 158,940 recipients involved. The studies are divided as to the sources of their effect upon helpees—the effect of training helpers or the effects of training helpees directly. In turn, the effects are divided by areas of functioning; living, learning and working areas. The studies of the effects of helpers upon helpees are 96 percent positive, while the indices are 92 percent positive. This means that various helpers (parents, counselors, teachers, employers) have constructive effects upon their helpees (children, counselees, students, employees) when trained in interpersonally based helping skills. The studies of the direct effects of training the helpees are also 96 percent positive while the indices are 92 percent positive. This means that trained helpees (children, counselees, students, employees) demonstrate constructive change or gain when trained in interpersonally based self-helping skills.

Overall, the studies show that the effects of interpersonal skills training upon helpers and the direct training upon helpees are 96 percent positive while the indices are 92 percent positive. This means that our chances of achieving any reasonable living, learning or working outcome are about 96 percent when either helpers or helpees are trained in interpersonally based helping skills. Conversely, the chances of achieving any human goal without trained helpers or helpees are random.

Together, the results of these studies constitute an answer to the challenges to the efficacy of the helping professions (Anthony, 1979; Eysenck, 1960, 1965; Levitt, 1963; Lewis, 1965).

Table 1:
A Summary of Interpersonal Skills Training Studies and Results Across Multiple Indices of Helpee Living, Learning and Working Outcomes*

	SOURCES OF EFFECT	
OUTCOME AREAS	HELPERS	HELPEES
LIVING	22 Studies 25,682 Helpees 91% Positive 114 Indices 83% Positive	35 Studies 2,279 Helpees 91% Positive 128 Indices 85% Positive
LEARNING	32 Studies 81,298 Learners 97% Positive 261 Indices 92% Positive	26 Studies 3,610 Learners 100% Positive 78 Indices 99% Positive
WORKING	22 Studies 33,836 Employees 96% Positive 81 Indices 92% Positive	27 Studies 12235 Employees 95% Positive 107 Indices 92% Positive
SUB-TOTAL	76 Studies 140,816 Recipients 96% Positive 456 Indices 92% Positive	88 Studies 18,124 Recipients 96% Positive 313 Indices 92% Positive
GRAND TOTAL	164 Studies 158,940 Recipients 96% Positive 769 Indices 92% Positive	

*(Carkhuff, 1983)

Helpee Outcomes

In early research, helpee outcomes emphasized the emotional changes or gains of the helpees. Since the helping methods were insight-oriented, the process emphasized helpee exploration, and the outcome assessments measured the changes in the helpee's level of emotional insights (Rogers et al., 1967; Truax & Carkhuff, 1967). Clearly, these emotional outcomes were restrictive because they were assessing only one dimension of the helpee's functioning.

These outcomes were later defined more broadly to incorporate all dimensions of human development to which the helping process is dedicated. The emotional dimension was extended to incorporate the interpersonal functioning of the helpees (Carkhuff, 1969, 1971 a, 1983, 1984). The dimension of physical functioning was added to measure relevant data on the helpees' fitness and energy levels (Collingwood, 1972). The intellectual dimension was added to measure the helpees' intellectual achievement and capabilities (Aspy & Roebuck, 1972, 1977).

In summary, helping effectiveness is a function of the helper's skills to facilitate the helping process to accomplish helping outcomes. Helping outcomes include the physical, emotional and intellectual dimensions of human development. The helping process, by which outcomes are accomplished, emphasizes the helpee's explorating, understanding and acting. The helping skills, by which the process is facilitated, include attending, responding, personalizing and initiating skills.

The Training Applications

It was a natural step to train helpers in helping skills and study the effects on helping outcomes. It was also only natural that the first training applications take place with credentialed counselors and therapists. Next came the training of lay and indigenous helper populations, followed by the direct training of helpee populations to service themselves.

Credentialed Helpers

The first series of training applications demonstrated that professional helpers could be trained to function at levels commensurate with "outstanding" practitioners (Truax & Carkhuff, 1967). In a later series, it was established that credentialed professionals could, in the brief time of 100 hours or less, learn to function above minimally effective and self-sustaining levels of interpersonal skills, levels beyond those offered by most "outstanding" practitioners (Carkhuff, 1969, 1983 a). Perhaps most importantly, trained counselors were able to involve their counselees in the helping process at levels that led to constructive change or gain. In one demonstration study in guidance, against a very low base success rate of 13 to 25 percent, the trained counselors were able to demonstrate success rates between 74 and 91 percent (Carkhuff & Berenson, 1976).

A series of training applications in teaching soon followed. Hefele (1971) found student achievement to be a function of systematic training of teachers in helping skills. Berenson (1971) found the experimentally-trained teachers were rated significantly higher in interpersonal skills and competency in the classroom than were other teachers who received a variety of control conditions. Aspy and Roebuck (1977), building upon their earlier work, have continued to employ a variety of teacher training strategies demonstrating the positive effects of helping skills upon student physical, emotional and intellectual functioning.

Functional Professionals

It is clear that a dimension such as interpersonal functioning is not the exclusive province of credentialed professionals. Lay personnel can learn as well as professionals to be empathic in their relations with helpee populations. With this growing recognition, a number of training applications using lay personnel were conducted. The majority of these programs dealt with staff personnel.

Staff personnel, such as nurses and hospital attendants, police and prison guards, dormitory counselors and community volunteers, were trained and their effects in treatment studied. The effects were very positive for both the staff and helpee populations for, after all, the line staff and helpee populations were those who lived most intimately with each other. In general, the lay helpers were able to elicit significant changes in work behaviors, discharge rates, recidivism rates and a variety of other areas including self-reports, significant-other-reports and expert-reports (Carkhuff, 1969, 1971 a, 1983; Carkhuff & Berenson, 1976).

Interpersonal-skills based training of managers and supervisors in business and industry has resulted in significant increases in worker productivity and cost avoidance. In training programs involving more than 2,000 managers and impacting nearly 25,000 employees, R.O.I.s (Return on Investment) ranged between 10:1 for one year to 30:1 for three years (Carkhuff, 1983,1984).

Indigenous Personnel

The difference between functional professional staff and indigenous functional professionals is the difference between the attendant and the patient, the police officer and the delinquent, the guard and the inmate, and the teacher and the student. That is to say, indigenous personnel are part of the community being serviced. It is a natural extension of the lay helper training principle to train helpee recipients as well as staff.

Here the research indicates that, with systematic selection and training, indigenous functional professionals can work effectively with the populations from which they are drawn. For example, human relations specialists drawn from recipient ranks have facilitated school and work adjustments for troubled populations. New careers teachers, themselves drawn from the ranks of the unemployed, have systematically helped others to learn the skills they needed in order to get and hold meaningful jobs (Carkhuff, 1971 a, 1983).

Helpee Populations

The logical culmination of helper training is to train helpee populations directly in the kinds of skills that they need to service themselves. Thus, parents of emotionally disturbed children were systematically trained in the skills that they needed to function effectively with themselves and their children (Carkhuff & Bierman, 1970). In another series of studies, patients were trained to offer each other rewarding human relationships. The results were significantly more positive than all other forms of treatment, including individual or group therapy, drug treatment or "total push" treatment (Pierce & Drasgow, 1969). Training was, indeed, the preferred mode of treatment!

The concept of training as treatment led directly to the development of programs to train entire communities to create a therapeutic milieu. This has been accomplished most effectively in institutional-type settings where staff and residents are trained in the kinds of skills necessary to work effectively with each other. Thus both institutional and community-based criminal justice settings have yielded data indicating reduced recidivism and increased employability (Bierman, et al., 1976; Carkhuff, 1974; Collingwood et al., 1978; Montgomery & Brown, 1980).

In summary, both lay staff and indigenous personnel may be selected and trained as functional professional helpers. In these roles, they can effect any human development that professionals can—and more! Further, teaching the helpee populations the kinds of skills that they need to service themselves is a direct extension of the helper principle. When we train people in the skills that they need to function effectively in their worlds, we increase the probability that they will, in fact, begin to live, learn and work in increasingly constructive ways.

Conclusions

In summary, training in interpersonal skills-based helping programs significantly increases the chances of our being effective in improving indices of helpee living, learning or working. Simply stated, trained helpers effectively elicit and use the input and feedback from the helpees concerning their helping effectiveness. Similarly, trained helpees learn to relate up, down and sideways in developing their own goals and programs.

We have found that all helping and human relationships may be "for better or for worse." The effects depend upon the helper's level of skills in facilitating the helpee's movement through the helping process toward constructive helping outcomes. These helping skills constitute the core of all helping experiences.

The helping skills may be used in all one-to-one and one-to-group relationships. They are used in conjunction with the helper's specialty skills. They may be used in conjunction with any of a number of potential preferred modes of treatment, drawn from a variety of helping orientations, to meet the helpee's needs. Finally, the same skills may be taught directly to the helpees in order to help them help themselves: teaching clients skills is the preferred mode of treatment for most helpee populations.

In conclusion, the helping skills will enable us to have helpful rather than harmful effects upon the people with whom we relate. We can learn to become effective helpers with success rates ranging upwards from two-thirds to over 90 percent, against a base success rate of around 20 percent. Most importantly, we can use these skills to help ourselves and others to become healthy human beings and to form healthy human relationships.

The Future of Helping

The future of helping lies in systematic approaches to human capital development. Operating proactively, we may develop guidance and preventative mental health training programs emphasizing youth development. Operating reactively, we may develop counseling, therapeutic and rehabilitation training programs which programmatically move from the helpees' frames of reference to observable and measurable physical, emotional and intellectual development. The key is helping skills—helping skills that facilitate the helpees' movement through exploring, understanding and acting. These helping skills emphasize interpersonal processing skills.

The future of helping also lies in the "morphing" of HRD models into human capital development of HCD models (Carkhuff, 2000). The principle difference between the two is the HCD emphasis upon intellectual processing: individual, interpersonal, interdependent. HCD emphasizes those resources that make us most important or capital in the 21st century.

Moreover, the future of helping is interdependently related to the future of science. When helping becomes a synergistic processing partner with the new science of possibilities (Carkhuff and Berenson, 2000 a, b) and its applications (Carkhuff and Berenson, 2000 a, b), then it will introduce both helpers and helpees to the realm of infinite possibilities: helpers will become *"scientist–artists"* who process interdependently with their helpee populations; helpees will become invaluable resources who are introduced to infinite possibilities.

APPENDIX D: REFERENCES

Adler, A. *Understanding Human Nature.* NY: Wolfe & Greenberg Publishers, 1927.

Alexik, M., and Carkhuff, R.R. The effects of the manipulation of client self-exploration upon high and low functioning counselors. *Journal of Clinical Psychology,* 1967, 23, 210–212.

Anthony, W.A. A methodological investigation of the "minimally facilitative level of interpersonal functioning." *Journal of Clinical Psychology,* 1971, 27, 156–57

Anthony, W.A. *The Principles of Psychiatric Rehabilitation.* Baltimore, MD: University Park Press, 1979.

Anthony, W.A., and Carkhuff, R.R. The functional professional therapeutic agent. In Gurman and Razin (Eds.), *Effective Psychotherapy: A Handbook of Research.* Oxford, England: Pergamon Press, 1978, pp. 103–119.

Anthony W.A., Cohen, M.R., and Vitalo, R. The measurement of rehabilitation outcome. *Schizophrenia Bulletin,* 1978, 4, 365–383.

Aspy, D.N. *Toward a Technology for Humanizing Education.* Champaign, IL: Research Press, 1973.

Aspy, D.N., and Roebuck, F.N. An investigation of the relationship between levels of cognitive functioning and the teacher's classroom behavior. *Journal of Educational Research,* May 1972.

Aspy, D.N., and Roebuck, F.N. *KIDS Don't Learn From People They Don't Like.* Amherst, MA: Human Resource Development Press, 1977.

Augelli, A., Handis, M., Brumbaugh, L., Hug, V., Shearer, R., Turner, D., and Frankel, J. Verbal helping behavior of experienced and novice telephone counselors. *Journal of Community Psychology,* 1978, 6, 222—228.

Authier, J., Gustafson, K., Guerney, B., and Kasdorf, J.A. The psychological practitioner as a teacher. *Counseling Psychologist,* 1975, 5, 31–50.

Bandler, R., and Grinder, J. *The Structure of Magic I & II.* Palo Alto, CA: Science and Behavior Books, 1975a.

Bandler, R., and Grinder, J. *Patterns of the Hypnotic Techniques of Milton H. Erickson, M.D.I.* Cupertino, CA: Meta Publications, 1975b.

Barker, L.L. *Listening Behavior.* Englewood Cliffs, NJ: Prentice-Hall, 1971.

Berenson, B.G., and Carkhuff, R.R. *Sources of Gain in Counseling and Psychotherapy.* NY: Holt, Rinehart & Winston, 1967.

Berenson, B.G., and Mitchell, K.M. *Confrontation: For Better or Worse.* Amherst, MA: Human Resource Development Press, 1974

Berenson, D.H. The effects of systematic human relations training upon the classroom performance of elementary school teachers. *Journal of Research and Development in Education,* 1971, 4, 70–85.

Berenson, D.H., Berenson, S.R., Berenson, B.G., Carkhuff, H.R., Griffin, A.H., and Ransom, B.M. The physical, emotional and intellectual effects of teaching learning skills to minority group drop-out learners. *Research Reports, Carkhuff Institute of Human Technology,* 1978, Vol. I, Number 3.

Bergin, A.E., and Garfield, S.L. (Eds.). *Handbook of Psychotherapy and Behavioral Change.* NY: John Wiley & Sons, 1971.

Binswanger, L. Existential analysis and psychotherapy. In F. Fromm-Reichmann and J.L. Moreno (Eds.), *Progress in Psychotherapy.* NY: Grune & Stratton, 1956.

Birdwhistell, R. Some body motion elements accompanying spoken American English. In L. Thayter (Ed.), *Communication: Concepts and Perspectives.* Washington, DC: Spartan, 1967.

Bierman, R. et al. *Toward Meeting Fundamental Human Service Needs.* Guelph, Ontario: Human Service Community, 1976.

Boss, M. *Daseinanalyses and Psychoanalysis.* New York: Basic Books, 1963.

Brammer, L. *The Helping Relationship.* Englewood Cliffs, NJ: Prentice-Hall, 1973.

Brammer, L. *The Helping Relationship.* 2nd ed. Englewood Cliffs, NJ: Prentice-Hall, 1979.

Brill, A.A. *The Basic Writings of Sigmund Freud.* New York: Random House, 1938.

Bucker, L. Joint effect of feedback and goal setting on performance: A field study of residential energy conservation. *Journal of Applied Psychology,* 1978, 63, 428–433.

Cannon, J.R., and Pierce, R.M. Order effects in the experimental manipulation of therapeutic conditions. *Journal of Clinical Psychology,* 1968, 24, 242–244.

Carkhuff, R.R. The differential functioning of lay and professional helpers. *Journal of Counseling Psychology,* 1968, 15, 117–126.

Carkhuff, R.R. *Helping and Human Relation, Volumes I & II.* NY: Holt, Rinehart & Winston, 1969. Amherst, MA: Human Resource Development Press, 1984.

Carkhuff R.R. *The Development of Human Resources.* NY: Holt, Rinehart & Winston, 1971 a. Amherst, MA: Human Resource Development Press, 1984.

Carkhuff, R.R. Training as a preferred mode of treatment. *Journal of Counseling Psychology,* 1971(b), 18, 123–131.

Carkhuff, R.R. *Cry Twice.* Amherst, MA: Human Resource Development Press, 1974.

Carkhuff, R.R. *Toward Actualizing Human Potential.* Amherst, MA: Human Resource Development Press, 1981.

Carkhuff, R.R. *Interpersonal Skills and Human Productivity.* Amherst, MA: Human Resource Development Press, 1983.

Carkhuff, R.R. *The Exemplar—The Exemplary Performer in the Age of Information.* Amherst, MA: Human Resource Development Press, 1984.

Carkhuff, R.R. *Productive Problem-Solving.* Amherst, MA: Human Resource Development Press, 1985 a.

Carkhuff, R.R. *Productive Program Development.* Amherst, MA: Human Resource Development Press, 1985 b.

Carkhuff, R.R. *Human Processing and Human Productivity.* Amherst, MA: Human Resource Development Press, 1986.

Carkhuff, R.R. *The Age of the New Capitalism.* Amherst, MA: Human Resource Development Press, 1988.

Carkhuff, R.R. *Empowering.* Amherst, MA: Human Resource Development Press, 1989.

Carkhuff, R.R. *HCD XXI—Human Capital Development in the 21st Century.* Amherst, MA: Human Resource Development Press, 2000.

Carkhuff, R.R., and Alexik, M. The differential effects of the manipulation of client self-exploration upon high and low functioning counselors. *Journal of Counseling Psychology,* 1967, 14, 350–355.

Carkhuff, R.R., and Anthony, W. A. *The Skills of Helping.* Amherst, MA: Human Resource Development Press, 1979.

Carkhuff, R.R., and Banks, G. Training as a preferred mode of facilitating relations between races and generations. *Journal of Counseling Psychology,* 1970, 17, 413–418.

Carkhuff, R.R., and Becker, J. *Toward Excellence in Education.* Amherst, MA: Carkhuff Institute of Human Technology, 1979.

Carkhuff R.R., and Berenson, B.G. *Beyond Counseling and Therapy.* NY: Holt, Rinehart & Winston, 1967, 1977.

Carkhuff, R.R., and Berenson, B.G. *Teaching as Treatment.* Amherst, MA: Human Resource Development Press, 1976.

Carkhuff, R.R., and Berenson, B.G. *The New Science of Possibilities. I. The Processing Science.* Amherst, MA: Human Resource Development Press, 2000 a.

Carkhuff, R.R., and Berenson, B.G. *The New Science of Possibilities. II. The Processing Technologies.* Amherst, MA: Human Resource Development Press, 2000 b.

Carkhuff, R.R., and Berenson, B.G. *The Possibilities Leader—The New Science of Possibilities Management.* Amherst, MA: Human Resource Development Press, 2000 c.

Carkhuff, R.R., and Berenson, B.G. *The Possibilities Organization—The New Science of Possibilities Management.* Amherst, MA: Human Resource Development Press, 2000 d.

Carkhuff, R.R., and Bierman, R. Training as a preferred mode of treatment of parents of emotionally disturbed children. *Journal of Counseling Psychology,* 1970, 17, 157–161

Carkhuff, R.R., and Pierce, R.M. *Helping Begins at Home.* Amherst, MA: Human Resource Development Press, 1976.

Carothers, J.E., and Inslee, L.J. Level of empathic understanding offered by volunteer telephone services. *Journal of Counseling Psychology,* 1974, 21, 274–276.

Collingwood, T. HRD Model and Physical fitness. In D.W. Kratochvil (Ed.), *HRD Model in Education.* Baton Rouge, LA: Southern University, 1972.

Collingwood, T., Douds, A., Williams, H., and Wilson, R. *Developing Youth Resources.* Amherst, MA: Carkhuff Institute of Human Technology, 1978.

Combs, A., Avila D., and Purkey, W. *Helping Relationships: Basic Concepts for the Helping Professions.* Boston, MA: Allyn and Bacon, 1978.

Conn, J. The rise and decline of psychoanalysis. *Psychiatric Opinion,* 1973, 10 (5), 34–38.

Danish, S., and Hauer, A. *Helping Skills: A Basic Training Program.* NY: Behavioral Publications, 1973.

Egan, G. *The Skilled Helper.* Monterey, CA: Brooks, Cole, 1975, 1990.

Ekman, P., Friesen, W., and Ellworth, P. *Emotion in the Human Face.* NY: Pergammon, 1972.

Erez, M. Feedback: A necessary condition for the goal-setting performance relationship. *Journal of Applied Psychology,* 1977, 62, 624–627.

Eysenck, H.J. The effects of psychotherapy. In H.J. Eysenck (Ed.), *The Handbook of Abnormal Psychology.* NY: Basic Books, 1960.

Eysenck, H.J. The effects of psychotherapy. *International Journal of Psychotherapy,* 1965, 1, 99–178.

Eysenck, H.J. New approaches to mental illness: The failure of a tradition. In H. Gottesfeld (Eds.), *The Critical Issues of Community Mental Health.* New York: Behavioral Publications, 1972.

Fischer, J., Pavenza, G.J., Kickertz, N.S., Hubbard, L.J., and Grayston, S.B. The relationship between theoretical orientation and therapist's empathy, warmth and genuineness. *Journal of Counseling Psychology,* 1975, 22, 399–403.

Flowers, J., and Goldman, R. Assertion training for mental health paraprofessionals. *Journal of Counseling Psychiatry,* 1976, 23, 147–150.

Freud, A. *Collected Papers.* London: Hogarth and The Institute of Psycho-Analysis, 1924.

Freud, S. *New Introductory Lectures.* NY: Norton, 1933.

Freund, J. Psychoanalysis: Uses and abuses. *Psycho-somatics,* 1972, 13 (6), 377–379.

Friedman, L. The struggle in psychotherapy: Its influence on some theories. *Psychoanalytic Review,* 1975, 62, 453–462.

Fromm, E. *Man for Himself.* NY: Holt, Rinehart & Winston, 1947.

Garfield, S. Research on client variables in psychotherapy. In A.E. Bergin and S.L. Garfield (Eds.), *Handbook of Psychotherapy and Behavioral Change.* NY: Wiley & Sons, 1971.

Gazda, G. *Human Relations Development.* Boston, MA: Allyn and Bacon, 1973.

Genther, R. Evaluating the functioning of community hot lines. *Professional Psychology,* 1974, 5(4), 409–414.

Genther, R., and Moughan, J. Introverts and extroverts' responses to non-verbal attending behavior. *Journal of Counseling Psychology,* 1977, 24,144–146.

Genther, R., and Saccuzzo, D. Accuracy of perceptions of psychotherapeutic content as a function of observers' levels of facilitation. *Journal of Clinical Psychology,* 1977, 33, 517–519.

Ginzberg, E., Ginsburg, S.W., Axelrod, S., and Herma, J.L. *Occupational Choice.* NY: Columbia University Press, 1951.

Goldstein, A., Sprafkin, R., and Gershaw, N. *Skill Training for Community Living.* NY: Pergammon Press, 1976.

Goodman, G. *Companionship Therapy.* San Francisco: Jossey-Bass, 1972.

Gordon, R. *Interviewing: Strategy, Techniques and Tactics.* Homewood, IL: Dorsey Press, 1975.

Griffin, A., Linder, J., Logan-EL, G. and Carkhuff, C. *Getting Away Clean—Skills for Handling Negative Peer Pressure.* Amherst, MA: Carkhuff Institute of Human Technology, 1987.

Guerney, B. *Relationship Enhancement.* San Francisco: Jossey-Bass, 1977.

Hackney, H., and Cornier, L. *Counseling Strategies and Objectives.* 2nd ed. Englewood Cliffs, NJ: Prentice-Hall, 1979.

Hall, E. *The Silent Language.* NY: Doubleday, 1959.

Hall, E. *Beyond Culture.* NY: Doubleday, 1976.

Hefele, T.J. The effects of systematic human relations training upon student achievement. *Journal of Research and Development in Education,* 1971, 4, 52–69.

Heidegger, M. *Being and Time.* London: SCM Press, 1962.

Holder, T., Carkhuff, R.R., and Berenson, B.G. The differential effects of the manipulation of therapeutic conditions upon high and low functioning clients. *Journal of Counseling Psychology,* 1967, 14, 63–66.

Holroyd, J., and Goldenberg, I. The use of goal attainment scaling to evaluate a ward treatment program for disturbed children. *Journal of Clinical Psychology,* 1978, 34, 732–739.

Homey, K. *Our Inner Conflicts.* NY: Norton, 1945.

Ivey, A. The counselor as teacher. *Personnel and Guidance Journal,* 1976, 54, 431–434.

Ivey, A., and Authier, J. *Microcounseling.* Springfield, IL: Thomas, 1971, 1978.

Johnson, D. *Reaching Out: Interpersonal Effectiveness and Self-Actualization.* Englewood Cliffs, NJ: Prentice-Hall, 1972.

Jones, E. *The Life and Work of Sigmund Freud.* New York: Basic Books, 1953.

Jung, C. *The Integration of the Personality.* NY: Holt, Rinehart & Winston, 1939.

Krasner, L., and Ullman, L. *Research in Behavior Modification.* NY: Holt, Rinehart & Winston, 1965.

Levitt, E.E. Psychotherapy with children: A further evaluation. *Behavior Research and Therapy,* 1963, 1, 45–51.

Lewis, W.W. Continuity and intervention in emotional disturbance: A review. *Exceptional Children,* 1965, 31, 465–475.

May, R. (Ed.). *Existential Psychology.* NY: Random House, 1961.

Mehrabian, A. *Nonverbal Communication.* NY: Aldine-Atherton, 1972.

Mickelson, D.J., and Stevic, R.R. Differential effects of facilitative and non-facilitative behavioral counselors. *Journal of Counseling Psychology,* 1971, 18, 314–319.

Montgomery, C., and Brown, A. *In the Land of the Blind.* Amherst, MA: Carkhuff Institute of Human Technology, 1980.

Mullahy, P. *Oedipus: Myth and Complex: A Review of Psychoanalytic Theory.* New York: Grove, 1948.

Murphy, H.B., and Rowe, W. Effects of counselor facilitative level on client suggestibility. *Journal of Counseling Psychology,* 1977, 24, 6–9.

Okun, B. *Effective Helping: Interviewing and Counseling Techniques.* North Scituate, MA: Duxbury Press, 1976.

Older, J. Four taboos that may limit the success of psychotherapy. *Psychiatry,* 1977, 40,197–203.

Pagell, W., Carkhuff, R.R., and Berenson, B.G. The predicted differential effects of the level of counselor functioning upon the level of functioning of out-patients. *Journal of Clinical Psychology,* 1967, 23, 510–512.

Parsons, F. *Choosing a Vocation.* Boston, MA: Houghton Mifflin, 1909.

Patterson C. *Theories of Counseling and Psychotherapy.* 2nd ed. NY: Harper & Row, 1973.

Piaget, G., Berenson, B.G., and Carkhuff, R.R. The differential effects of the manipulation of therapeutic conditions by high and low functioning counselors upon high and low functioning clients. *Journal of Consulting Psychology,* 1967, 31, 481–486.

Pierce, R.M., and Drasgow, J. Teaching facilitative interpersonal functioning to psychiatric inpatients. *Journal of Counseling Psychology,* 1969,16, 295–298.

Rank, O. *The Trauma of Birth.* NY: Harcourt, 1929.

Reed, S., Roberts, M., and Forehand, R. Evaluation of effectiveness of standardized parent training programs in altering the interaction of mothers and non-compliant children. *Behavior Modification,* 1977, 1, 323–350.

Rogers, C., Gendlin, E., Keisler, D., and Truax, C. *The Therapeutic Relationship and Its Impact.* Westport, CT: Greenwood Press, 1967.

Rosenbaum, A., and Calhoun, J. The use of the telephone hotline in crisis intervention: A review. *Journal of Community Psychology,* 1977, 5, 325–339.

Schefflen, A. *Stream and Structure of Communication Behavior.* Bloomington, IN: Purdue University Press, 1969.

Schulman, E. *Intervention in Human Services.* St. Louis: Mosby, 1974.

Schultz, J.L. Hotlines: Is concern enough? *The Vocational Guidance Quarterly,* 1975, 23 (4), 367–368.

Smith, D.L. Goal attainment scaling as an adjunct to counseling. *Journal of Counseling Psychology,* 1976, 23, 22–27.

Smith-Hanen, S. Nonverbal behavior and counselor warmth and empathy. *Journal of Counseling Psychology,* 1977, 24, 84–91.

Sprinthall, N., and Mosher, R. Psychological education: A means to promote personal development during adolescence. *The Counseling Psychologist,* 1971, 2(4), 3–84.

Sue, S., McKinney, H., and Allen, D.G. Predictors of the duration of therapy for clients in the community mental health center system. *Community Mental Health Journal,* 1976,12, 374–376.

Sue, S., McKinney, H., Allen, D.B., and Hall, I. Delivery of community mental health services to black and white clients. *Journal of Consulting and Clinical Psychology,* 1974, 43, 794–801.

Sullivan, H. The meaning of anxiety in psychiatry and life. *Psychiatry,* 1948,11(1).

Super, D.E. *Appraising Vocational Fitness.* NY: Harper & Row, 1949.

Truax, C.B., and Carkhuff, R.R. The experimental manipulation of therapeutic conditions. *Journal of Consulting Psychology,* 1965, 29,119–124.

Truax, C.B., and Carkhuff, R.R. *Toward Effective Counseling and Psychotherapy.* Chicago, IL: Aldine, 1967.

Vitalo, R. The effects of facilitative interpersonal functioning in a conditioning paradigm. *Journal of Counseling Psychology,* 1970,17,141–144.

Vitalo, R. Teaching improved interpersonal functioning as a preferred mode of treatment. *Journal of Clinical Psychology,* 1971, 27,166–170.

Walker, R.A. The ninth panacea: Program evaluation. *Evaluation,* 1972, 1 (1), 45–53.

Watson, J.B. Behaviorism and the concept of mental disease. *Journal of Philosophical Psychology,* 1916, 13, 589–597.

Wilier, B., & Miller, G. On the relationship of client satisfaction to client characteristics and outcome of treatment. *Journal of Clinical Psychology,* 1978, 34,157–160.

Wolkon, G.W. Characteristics of clients and continuity of care into the community. *Community Mental Health Journal,* 1970, 6, 215–221.

Wolpe, J., Salter, A., and Renya, L. *The Conditioning Therapies.* NY: Holt, Rinehart & Winston, 1964.

INDEX

312